Dr John Coleman

THE CLUB OF ROME
THE THINK TANK OF THE NEW WORLD ORDER

ⒸMNIA VERITAS.

John Coleman

John Coleman is a British author and former member of the Secret Intelligence Service. Coleman has produced various analyses of the Club of Rome, the Giorgio Cini Foundation, Forbes Global 2000, the Interreligious Peace Colloquium, the Tavistock Institute, the Black Nobility and other organisations with New World Order themes.

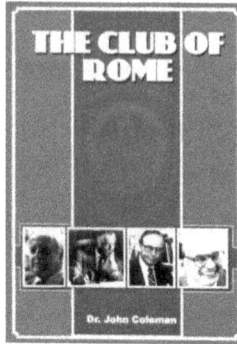

THE CLUB OF ROME
The Think Tank of the New World Order

The Club of Rome (COR) is the chief "think tank" for the New World Order that was unknown in America until exposed by Dr. Coleman in 1969 for the very first time and published under the same title in 1970. Set up on the orders of the Committee of 300, its existence was denied until the silver anniversary celebrations of its founding held in Rome 25 years later. The COR plays a vital role in all U.S. government planning, internal and external. It has nothing to do with Rome, Italy or the Catholic Church.

CHAPTER 1

ECHOES OF THE FRENCH REVOLUTION

In order to begin to understand world events, it is necessary for us to realize that the many tragic and explosive events of the 20th century did not just happen by themselves; but that they were planned according to a well laid out blueprint. Who were the planners and creators of significant events?

The creators of these often violent and revolutionary events belong in the main to secret societies that infest our world, just as they have always done. Mostly, these secret societies are based upon the occult and occult practices, but as with all secret societies to make up secret governments, they are controlled by the Committee of 300. Those poorly informed persons, who believe that devil worship, demons and witchcraft have vanished from modern society, are misinformed. Today, occult-based secret societies along with Luciferianism, Black Magic and Voodoo, are flourishing and appear to be far more widespread than was originally thought.

It is the tolerating of these secret societies in our midst, many of whose principals pose as Christians, added to our permissible attitude toward these organizations and their leaders who are the cause of our problems, national and international. Every unrest, revolution and war can inevitably be traced back to one or another or a combination of several secret societies. Secrecy indicates a problem, for if the secret societies were working for the good of the individual and the state, why the need for such profound secrecy in which they cloak themselves, their organizations and their deeds? I recall that the practice of voodoo, attributed to black Africa, really sprang from Jethro, the Ethiopian. Like Voodoo, most occult practices and their attendant secret societies are anti-Christian, and they make no apology for it, although some in Freemasonry try to dissemble or hide their anti-Christian teachings.

Yet, to their credit, Masons realize that Christ was far more than a religious leader. Masons believe that Christ came to change the face of the world and that He set His face against secret societies. That is why so many secret societies turn their adherents against Christianity. Right from the moment Christ began his ministry, Gnosticism sprang up in opposition to the perfect ideals of Christianity. Christ warned the world that we wrestle not against flesh and blood, but against the forces of darkness and spiritual wickedness in high places. What this means is that the bottom line of our struggle against Communism, Marxism, Socialism, Liberalism and a One World Government is a spiritual one. Show me a secret society and I will show you a Christ-hating occult theocracy. Christ said: **"Know the truth and the truth shall make you free."**

Note that Christ used the word "shall," which is much stronger than "will." Christ was talking about the people who were in bondage to secret societies—as they are today—the ordinary people who are despised by the leaders of occult theocracies, who have no use for them, other than as servants and slaves.

These leaders think it perfectly normal to kill off millions of people they consider as "surplus to their requirements." This evil "kill" philosophy has crept into the U.S. military through men like Richard Cheney, Donald Rumsfeld, Richard Perle and Paul Wolfowitz. It is a thoroughly alien concept that does not belong in a Republican form of Government. The leaders of evil secret societies threaten our entire civilization. Some of the secret cults who are very active in our affairs today are Gnosticism, the cult of Dionysus and the subject of this work, the cult of the Club of Rome. But I must return to the starting point of this work, which is found in modern history under the heading of "The French Revolution."

Modern history books do not teach that the so-called French Revolution had its roots in England, where a demonist, William Petty, the Earl of Shelburne, trained economists Malthus and Adam Smith of the British East India Company (BEIC), and mass murderers Danton and Marat. After their time spent with Shelburne in England, Danton and Marat were spirited to Paris to be unleashed upon an unsuspecting and defenseless French people and the monarchy, in an orgy of blood lust. Years later, Lord Alfred Milner was to unleash Lenin on an unsuspecting Christian Russia in an almost carbon copy of the French Revolution.

The driving force behind the French Revolution was a secret society called the Illuminati, orchestrated by the London Qator Coronati Freemason Lodge in London, and the Nine Sisters Freemason (Orient) Lodge of Paris. A brief history of the Illuminati is essential if we are to understand how the Club of Rome came to be constituted. There is disagreement concerning the origins of the Illuminati, but there is also a good deal of agreement that the Illuminati sprang from the Rosicrucians, the so-called master holders of abundant secrets such as the Philosopher's Stone, which Rosicrucians say they received from the ancient Chaldeans, the Magi and the Egyptian priesthood.

Rosicrucian's say they can protect human life by the use of certain nostrums and also claim to be able to restore youth. They are also known by the title, "the Immortals," and teach that all mysteries have been revealed to them. In their earlier days, they were known as the "Invisible Brothers," and later as, "The Rosicrucian Brethren." A branch of the Rosicrucians calls itself, "The Rite of Swedenborg," or the "Illuminati of Stockholm," which was founded in 1881 by Emmanuel Swedenborg, a Master Mason, whose signature is still on the list of members of the Lodge of Lund, Sweden, where Swedenborg was born. The Rite of Swedenborg is merely a modification of the Order of the Illuminati of Abingdon, established in 1783. Then, as now, it was the cream of royalty, titled nobility and high society who were the leaders of this secret order. But the main Order of Illuminati was founded in Bavaria on May 1, 1776, by one Adam Weishaupt, professor of Canon Law at the University of Ingolstadt.

Weishaupt was a product of Jesuit education, and the Illuminati bear a close resemblance to the Order of the Golden Cross. Here again, Illuminism is clearly tied in with Masonry, the Order of the Rosicrucian's, the Templars—or Order of French Masonic Degrees. Behind of all these orders stood Moses Mendelsohn, a student of the Kabal, with his stated objective to move to establish a One World Government-New World Order. The principal business of the Illuminati was, and is, carrying on war against Christianity, which battle it carries out through shameful accusations against the life and teachings of Christ. Politically speaking, Illuminism is working to overthrow the existing order of all governments, more especially those who practice the Christian religion. Its members are pledged to blind obedience to their superiors and their secret, revolutionary plans to bring about the New World Order, which first went into operation with the French Revolution.

Illuminati plans to destroy the Christian monarchy of France were discovered when an Illuminati messenger by the name of Jacob Lang was killed by lightning as he rode his horse to deliver revolutionary instructions to the Bavarian lodges. Subsequently, Lang's papers fell into the hands of the Bavarian authorities, and later, an iron box full of papers giving details of the coming plot against France was also discovered. Illuminism was introduced to France by the Marquis de Mirabeau and then adopted by the Duc de Orleans, Grand Master of Orient Freemasonry in France. By the way, it was decided to induct Talleyrand as one of the most notable figures of his day, into Illuminism. One of the acts of putridity performed by adherents of Order of the Illuminati is castration. Janos Kadar, the former dictator of Hungry, publicly announced that he had actually had this rite performed on him.

CHAPTER 2

CROWLEY, PIKE AND MAZZINI

Neither Freemasonry nor Illuminism has died out. There are those in intelligence circles who believe both to be stronger now than they were at the time of the French Revolution.

The death of Illuminist/Mason world leaders, Guiseppe Mazzini and Albert Pike, did not signal any change in growth and direction of either organization.

No doubt there will be some who will be offended by my references to Masonry. I do not mean to cause offense to Masons. I am merely trying to present a true account of how and why certain events occur in the world.

American Masons claim quite erroneously that their Masonry differs from European Masonry. Let me correct the error: The Rosicrucian cabalists, Leon Templer and Jacob Leon, jointly designed the English Grand Lodge of Masonry, as well as its emblem.

This is a very definite tie between Anglo-Saxon Masonry and the occult European Grand Orient masonry. I say, "occult," because that is what the great German General Ludendorff called it. The connection between European Rosicrucian Masonry and American Masonry was always close, and remains so to this day.

The three main Masonic rites are:

> The Scottish Rite of Freemasonry which has 33 degrees.

> The Rite of Mizraim, or Egyptian Rite, with 96 degrees.

> The Orient Rite which is basically the one followed by European masonry.

John Harker, author of *Grand Mystic Temple*, stated as follows:

> *We the English have thus joined with the Scottish Rite, allied with the Mizraem, and now with Memphis. In the case of the former, we established relations with various supreme grand councils and revised the statutes of 1862 in preference to the forged constitution of 1786, in the year 1884, in Mizraem, with the old bodies of Naples and Paris and Memphis with America, Egypt, Romania and various bodies working that Rite. We also in these three Rites accepted foreign charters to confirm our original powers.*

This should dispose of the mistaken belief often quoted by American Masons that Anglo-Saxon Masonry has nothing to do with European Masonry. Harker should have known, after all, as he was the Grand Mystic.

On November 11, 1912, Harker was elected Grand Imperial Master, a degree higher than the 96th degree of the Rite of Mizraïm. After his death in 1913, Harker was succeeded first by Henry Mayer and then by Alistair Crowley, 33rd,

90th and 96th Degree Patriot Grand Master. Thus it is clear that American Masons are part and parcel of European Masonry, whether they know it or not, and the truth is, most do not. Crowley was one of the most beastly figures in the history of secret societies; a man who was to greatly influence the policies of the Club of Rome (COR.)

Crowley was fond of quoting Malthus and Adam Smith, servants of the British East India Company (BEIC) today known as the **Committee of 300.** Both men played a leading role in the concerted drive by King George III to ruin the American colonists through the one-way street of "free trade."

Malthus and Smith became "favorite sons" of the COR. It is very easy to see the connecting link between the plans of the BEIC and the present policies of the COR, particularly in the COR "Post Industrial Zero-Growth" policies to put an end to the industrial dominance of the United States. The basic religion followed by the Club of Rome is Gnosticism and the cult of the Bogomils and Catharis. Members of the British monarchy are firm believers in these "religions" and in the main, it is accurate to say that certainly, the royal family members are not Christians. It is also quite easy to see the connection to the **"Committee of 300."**

Crowley is believed to have taken part in more than 150 ritual murders, an important part of occult demonology. Most of the victims were children, slain with a silver knife. Such bestialities continue to this very day, which may account for the large number of missing children who are never found. Crowley is still greatly admired by COR hierarchy, as he was by several of the leading British figures in the atom spy case. Anthony Blunt, the Keeper of the Queen's Art (a very high title) before he was unmasked as a KGB agent, was a great devotee of Crowley. The bottom line is that Masonry starting at the *Knights of Kadosh* degree is an ongoing revolt against the existing order of things and dedicated to the overthrow of Christianity and the Republic of the United States of America—as indeed is the COR. As long as Masonry continues to flourish in our midst, for so long will chaos and unrest continue, for that is the intent and purpose of all revolutionary secret societies. The modern Club of Rome is but an ongoing, unbroken succession of secret societies that have as their goal, the destruction of liberty and freedom, which happened in the period we now know as the Dark Ages. Thus, it may be safely assumed that the COR is a New World Order-One World Government project designed to facilitate a swifter transition to universal slavery known as the New Dark Age, under the control of the **Committee of 300.**

CHAPTER 3

WHAT IS THE CLUB OF ROME?

The very name was chosen to deceive the unwary, because the Club of Rome has nothing to do with the Vatican or the Catholic Church. While the evildoers work night and day, Christian America slumbers on. When I wrote the First Edition of this work back in 1970, only a handful of people in intelligence knew of the existence of this, the most powerful secret society in the hands of the Committee of 300.

The Club of Rome consists of the oldest members of the so-called Black Nobility of Europe, decedents of the ancient families, who owned, controlled and ran Genoa and Venice in the 12th century. They are called "Black Nobility" because of their use of dirty tricks, murder, terrorism, unethical behavior, and worship of Satan—"black" deeds. They never hesitated to use force against anyone who dared to stand in their way, and this is no less true today than it was during the 13th to the 18th Centuries.

The Venetian Black Nobility is closely allied with the so-called German Marshall Fund, another name—like the Club of Rome—chosen to deceive the unwary. The Venetian Black Nobility consists of the richest and most ancient of all European families, their wealth far surpassing that of the Rockefellers, for instance, and they are part of the

Committee of 300, the most powerful controlling body in the world. One of the oldest of the Venetian Black Nobility dynasties is the Guelph dynasty. Queen Elizabeth II, for instance, is a Black Guelph—her great grandmother Victoria descended from that family. The Black Nobility and European royalty are prominent members of the COR, which has as its objective, the dissolution of the United States as an industrial and agricultural power. Its other goals are not so readily visible and of a more complex nature, so I shall begin with the details of the COR's special conference and detail what was said and who said it.

As if to show their utter contempt for the election victory of Ronald Reagan in the November of 1980 elections, the group chose to meet in Washington, D.C. According to minutes of the meeting secretly recorded by an intelligence officer, the agenda was about how best to dismember the industrial heart of the United States and get rid of what one delegate referred to as, "the surplus population." This was consistent with the blueprint of Sir Bertrand Russell, as openly laid out in his book, *The Impact of Science on Society*. Other discussions dealt with methods to be used to gain control of the internal affairs of the United States. As several of the delegates came from the old Black Nobility families, or had worked for them for years, the dirty tricks, sedition, terror-tactics that were discussed, represented a direct challenge to the government and the people of the United States.

The problem was that the American people knew nothing of this meeting of dangerous satraps of the Black Nobility, and the jackals of the media were not about to enlighten them about the intent and purpose of the conclave. It was one of the best-kept secrets of all time. The conference was initiated and financed by the German Marshall Fund, which consists of the inner-core members of the WWII Morgenthau Planning Group, who are themselves under the control of three or four members of the venerable Order of St. John of Jerusalem.

This was the organization that originated the plan to de-industrialize post-war Germany, partition it, and turn what was left of the country into agricultural land. The attempted total eradication of the German nation originated with Morgenthau, a Zionist and a violent hater of Germany. The German Marshall Fund drew its vast resources from the companies of the Committee of 300 and the Wall Street and City of London international bankers, the very same crowd who bankrolled the Bolshevik Revolution which established the largest slave state on earth, and resulted in the verified deaths of millions of Christians, as chronicled by the notable writer, Alexander Solzhenitsyn. The chairman of the German Marshall Fund was David Rockefeller, no stranger to funding revolutionary groups of every color and stripe, ever since he and his family gained wealth and prominence.

The COR conference agenda included the best ways to nullify the Reagan Presidency, which had come as something of a surprise to the Club's members. Emphasis was laid on blocking the economic recovery promised by then candidate Reagan. In order to accomplish this, the delegates were told that the Democrat Party had to be radicalized. There is no such thing a "Democratic Party." There cannot be a Democratic Party in a Confederated Republic or a Constitutional Republic, which is what the U.S. is. It was suggested that the best way to Socialize President-elect Reagan, was to drive out conservative members of his inner circle and then turn the Democrats into a strong anti- capitalist Socialist party along the lines laid down by the Communist Manifesto of 1848. (The Capital Gain Tax was passed in 1989 as a direct result of COR planning).

In fact, since 1980, the Democrat Party have assumed the role of the Socialist/Communist Party and should be called, "The Socialist/Communist Party of the United States." Among those in attendance at the 1980 Washington meeting was Anthony Wedgewood Benn, leader of the British Socialists and chief Fabian Socialist strategist. Benn talked about the task of drawing up a comprehensive contingency plan for this purpose, to which he added a proposed "class war" between Reagan and the American people. One month after their first meeting, the Club of Rome plotters returned to Washington for a second conference. The meeting heard from a delegate representing the so-called conservative *Heritage Foundation,* a Washington—based "think tank" funded by brewery magnate Joseph Coors.

Heritage subsequently acted as the de facto employment agency for the Reagan Presidency, submitting a list of 3000 names of people it deemed suitable to fill key Reagan administration positions. Most of Heritage's recommendations were Liberals and far left of Marx career Socialists.

In 1980, Heritage Foundation was controlled from behind the scenes by arch-Fabian Socialist, Sir Peter Vickers Hall, whose antecedents belonged to the Milner Group. (It will be recalled that Milner was the instigator of the cruel war of genocide, the Anglo-Boer War fought to gain control of the gold and diamonds in South Africa.) Other prominent Socialists in attendance were the late Willy Brandt, a leading European contact for the KGB, and the late Olaf Palme, Francoise Mitterrand, then unemployed, but soon to be returned to power in France by the Committee of 300, Philip Agee, a renegade ex- CIA officer, Bettino Craxi, a leading Italian Socialist, Michael Harrington of the Institute of Democratic Social Studies in Washington, D.C. and an unknown Spanish Socialist by the name of Felipe Gonzalez, who had stopped over in Havana to consult with Castro before flying on to Washington.

The COR appointed Gonzalez as its case officer for Nicaragua and El Salvador, and it would be interesting to know just how involved Gonzalez became in the wars in Central and Latin America, in which Castro had a hand. More than 2000 delegates attended this amazing gathering, yet it was completely blacked out by the media. It is a tribute to my intelligence connections, that within 3 days of the meeting, in November of 1980, I was in possession of full documentation of this unholy watershed meeting of Socialist leaders. COR delegates attended what they perceived was the funeral oration of the United States, and among the Americans in attendance—apart from Agee and Harrington—were Jerry Rifkin, Gar Apelrovich of the Institute for Policies Studies (IPS), the most prominent Socialists in the country,) Ron Dellums of California and Gloria Steinham, organizer of the Women's Lib/ERA counterculture derived from the writings of Madame Kollontei, the Communist leader who toured the United States in the 1920s–1930s. Together, the delegates were as destructive a crew as could be mustered. Many of the leading delegates taking part, other than Palme, Brandt and Benn, were members of the Socialist International who met in daily sessions with State Department officials including Cyrus Vance and Henry Kissinger.

In case it is not known, the Socialist International is a particularly dangerous, subversive organization, which fully supports legalization of drugs and pornography as "destabilization tools," to be used against the United States. Details of the discussions were never made public, but according to the documents with which I was provided, the COR planned to isolate the United States, leaving open a single channel to the worst elements in the State Department and the KGB. Here was a situation that smacked of treason and sedition, not to mention conspiracy charges that should have been filed against those who attended the two COR meetings.

Apparently, a full day was devoted to how best to implement Lord Russell's plan to stifle industry and rid the world of more than 2 billion "useless eaters." It was resolved to redouble efforts to end construction of nuclear power stations and promote the policy of zero growth in conformity with the Adam Smith and Malthus economic theories and the writings of Russell. (See my coming book, "Nuclear Power.")

The Socialist International (SI) has long championed the idea of breaking up large cities and moving the population into smaller, more manageable (i.e., more easily controlled) towns and the countryside.

The first experiment in this regard was carried out by the Pol Pot regime in Cambodia, with the knowledge of Thomas Enders, a high-ranking U.S. State Department official.

CHAPTER 4

CONNECTION TO GLOBAL GENOCIDE

The Club of Rome, like the SI is strongly anti-national and favors the suppression of scientific development in the United States, Britain and Europe, and latterly, Japan. COR is believed to have maintained some connections with terrorist organizations like the Red Brigades.

This was implemented through arch-Socialist Bettino Craxi, a former leading player in the COR and a man known by intelligence agencies in France and Germany, to have had contacts in the Bader-Meinhoff gang, a notorious band of thugs who robbed banks and kidnapped public figures for ransom.

It was Craxi, who repeatedly tried to break the resolve of the Italian government not to negotiate with the Red Brigades for the release of kidnapped U.S. General Dozier.

Craxi was very close to Richard Gardner, a Committee of 300 executive, and Henry Kissinger. Gardner married into the Luccatti family, one of the most powerful of the Venetian Black Nobility families, known for centuries as able performers of dirty tricks and terrorism.

Neither Craxi nor the former Prime Minister of France,

Francois Mitterrand held official positions in 1980, but as I reported in several issues of World in Review (WIR) in 1971, Craxi was destined to play a leading role in Italian politics, and Mitterrand was to be returned to power in France—courtesy of the Club of Rome.

These predictions and that of Gonzalez later proved to be 100 percent accurate. The December 5, 1980 follow-up to the original COR meeting in Washington D.C., endorsed and accepted the COR's *Global 2000 Report—a blueprint for global genocide.* The report called for the death of 2 billion people by the year 2010 (hence the title). There is much evidence to tie the plan into several catastrophic events that are taking place throughout the world, like the recent disastrous earthquake in China.

The second conference also adopted the policy of euthanasia as policy for getting rid of the growing population of elderly people, and the delegates enthusiastically adopted the Russell term, "useless eaters," as a code word to describe millions of people who, in the eyes of the COR, are "surplus to requirements."

There are some who may consider "depopulation" of blacks, Asians and other colored races as a good idea. "There are far too many Indians (Asian Indians), Chinese and blacks already," a man wrote me, "so why are you against this?"

The truth is that it is not only these races that are slated to be culled; the "surplus to requirements" industrial workers in the United States are also the targets of the Global 2000 Report. Delegates to both COR meetings, one after another, expressed confidence in the ability to successfully promote their plans.

Twenty-fifth anniversary celebrations held in Germany in December of 1993 were to mark what had been achieved thus far.

It was also a personal vindication for me, because when I first revealed the existence of the COR in 1969, I was mocked and laughed to scorn. "The whole idea is the figment your overripe imagination," one man wrote. Another said. "Where is the documentation for your Club of Rome Report?" So momentous was the December of 1980 meeting that one would have thought the media would have done everything in its power to get a scoop. But this was not to be. The media threw a blanket of silence over the proceedings, with not a mention of it in the conventional press or on radio and television. This is called "freedom of the press"—American style. The American people are the most lied to, connived and cheated people in the world. We are also the most censored people—in this case, censorship by omission.

What did the delegates want? Michael Harrington explained it: "Willy Brandt wants social upheaval in Europe," and we should remember that the present social upheaval taking place in Germany is part of that plan. It is no accident. We should not think that social upheaval will not come to the United States.

The COR had the cooperation of the most Socialist government America has ever had; the Carter administration, which is dedicated to implementing the Communist Manifesto of 1848, as we saw in the Carter foreign policy which sat the blaze of revolution in South

Africa, the Philippines, Iran, Central America and South Korea. President Clinton and G.W. Bush picked up the mantel as we saw in Yugoslavia.

Poland was destabilized through the removal of President Gereck, which was arranged by Richard Gardner, the former U.S. ambassador to Rome.

One of the principal achievements arising out of the COR meeting was the pressure applied to President Reagan to retain the service of the Bank of International Settlements representative in the U.S., Paul Volcker, as head of the illegal Federal Reserve Banks. The Federal Reserve is not a U.S. Government institution, well-described by Louis T. McFadden, who called it "the greatest swindle in history."

It was Anthony Wedgewood-Benn, a very prominent Labor leader in Britain who insisted on the retention of Volcker, notwithstanding Reagan's campaign promises to rid America of the Volcker scourge. Benn felt that Volcker was the best man to bring "class war" to America. Benn nominated Rifkin to assist Volcker in this endeavor, which he said, "will polarize the Americans." The COR adopted a plan to destabilize currency through higher, and constantly fluctuating interest rates.

They wanted to get rid of Helmut Schmidt, then Chancellor of Germany, because he had been instrumental in stabilizing international interest rates. Sir Peter Vickers Hall called for interest rates in the United States to be hiked to 20 percent, as the best way to end capital investments in industry. Volcker was careful not to show his face at the COR meeting, but it is believed that he was briefed by Hall of the Heritage Foundation. Stuart Butler, who was chief executive officer at Heritage, had this to say to the COR delegates:

> In the Reagan administration we have a right-wing government that will impose some radical left-wing ideas. There is no reason why Communists, anarchists, libertarians or religious sects (he was talking about Satanism, Voodoo, Black Magic, witchcraft etc.) should not put their philosophies forward.

Butler suggested the old Socialist doctrine of "free enterprise zones" be pushed onto the Reagan administration. Free enterprise zones are found in places like Manila and Hong Kong, not to mention Mainland China. They are literally, "slave shops."

Butler called for free enterprise zones to be established in areas where industries had been uprooted and destroyed. Butler envisaged silent steel mills, shuttered machine tool factories and closed shipyards.

Cottage-type "industries" so common in Hong Kong would be a suitable means of employment for displaced persons from depopulated cities, according to the Post Industrial Zero Growth plan.

CHAPTER 5

MEN ARE LIKE INSECTS

I knew that not many readers were going to pay attention to this warning, written in 1981 a promise of a boom under the Reagan administration. But remember, nobody believed the documents that were found on the body of Lange, messenger of the Illuminati. The crowned heads of Europe were not in any mood to listen to "scare reports" issued by the Bavarian government about the Illuminati's plans for a bloody upheaval in France! People do not like their equanimity disturbed. As pointed out earlier, the COR represents the command structure of the Illuminati and the 13 top Illuminati families in the United States. Remember that the French Revolution Jacobin plan called for the murder of millions of "surplus to requirements" French nationals, especially Breton Celtic Christians who bore the brunt of the savagery. With that in mind, the statement made by Mitterrand at the COR meeting in December of 1980 is not to be taken lightly:

> *Industrial capitalist development is the enemy and the opposite of freedom.*

By that Mitterrand meant industrial development has given people a better life through cooperation, i.e. industrial development, and when people have a better life they are inclined to have larger families. Therefore, industrial capitalist development is the "enemy of freedom," simply because large areas of cooperation (industrial development) are prone to consume more of their (the Committee of 300) natural resources. This was the twisted logic behind the Club of Rome policies.

In a follow-up COR meeting held in Paris in March of 1982, Aurellio Peccei, founder of the Club, made the following statement:

> Men are like insects. They proliferate too much... It is about time to put on trial the concept of nation states obstacles to world culture. Christianity makes proud men; a mercantile society, which creates nothing but dead culture and classical music, oppressive signs on paper.

Whether believed or not, my paper is intended as a warning to the citizens of the United States that the equivalent of the Jacobin terror mobs will be unleashed upon our unsuspecting nation in due time. Jacobin-style mobs will be employed to bring about drastic changes in the way that we live in America, changes which could last for as long as a thousand years.

The COR's policy is *fewer and fewer people, consuming less and less and requiring less services, by whatever means.* It is a complete reversal of our society where more and more people demand better goods, services and life style, which is the essence of a productive society in a republican form of government. Significantly, Peccei said nothing about the one occult theocracy which passes itself off as a religion, but which it is not, being a political and economic system designed to control the lives of men, down to the last detail, as we saw in the Bolshevik Revolution. Peccei and the Club of Rome are the successors of the

French and Bolshevik Revolutions, the Socialists, Illuminati and the myriads of secret societies that are seeking to transform the United States into a slave-state, which they euphemistically call, a democracy. The United States is a Confederated Republic or a Constitutional Republic. It can never be a democracy, which has a long history as the wrecker of free societies.

As our Founding Fathers once said, *every pure democracy in history has been a total failure,* and they did not intend that the United States should end up as a failed democracy.

Club of Rome delegates undertook to prevent deployment of U.S. nuclear missiles in Europe, the fulfillment of which we saw on December 5, 1981. Hundreds of COR-instigated "Jacobin" mobs took to the streets of Paris and Hamburg: there were riots and civil commotions, which went on for several days and nights.

Note: Mob action succeeded in 1989. Because France's Giscard d'Estaing favored a nuclear umbrella for Europe, the COR disposed of him and replaced him with Socialist Mitterrand. One of Mitterrand's leading advisers was Jacques Attali, an occultist, who believed in suicide: *In a democratic society, the right to commit suicide is the most fundamental of human rights.* This is consistent with Peccei's beliefs that man is some kind of an accident within creation and that the majority of the world's population groups are not needed and should not have their views considered. This is the type of occult theocracy that thrived in Egypt, Judea and Syria and in many other parts of the ancient world, in which the cult of Dionysus played such an important role. It emerged very clearly from Club of Rome meetings that its main purpose and objective was to:

- retard industrial development,
- hold back scientific research,
- depopulate cities, especially the formerly industrialized cities of North America,
- move population to rural areas,
- cull the population of the world by at least 2 billion people,
- prevent reorganization of political forces who oppose COR plans,
- destabilize the United States through massive layoffs and loss of jobs and class and racial wars,
- destroy capital incentive through high interest rates and high capital gains taxes.

Now, for the doubters, who find my report "bizarre," and "far— fetched," as has been said of this work, take a look at the bills that have been passed by the House and Senate since this group met in November and December of 1980, and subsequently, on December 5, 1981. Because the media has subjected Americans to intense censorship—whether by omission or commission ~ does not make this report inaccurate and fanciful. It is worth remembering that when, the Jekyll Island plotters met to bring about a coup d'etat against our monetary system in America, which they later called the Federal Reserve Act, nobody knew about it—the press covered the banker's tracks and the innocent American nation went on as if nothing untoward was happening. The same set of conditions applies to COR planning.

The ultimate aim of Florence Kelley's legislative action was to Socialize America, and it began to take shape with frightening speed under the administration of Franklin D. Roosevelt and James Earl Carter. Florence Kelly was a notable Fabian Socialist from whom Roosevelt sought and obtained advice that went into the making of many of his policy decisions. Looking back, we see that large areas of our industrial heartland have been laid waste, 40 million industrial workers are permanently laid off, and racial conflicts are a daily occurrence. There are also many Socialist bills that impinge directly on the future of this great country, agricultural bills designed to rob the American farmer of his lands, "crime" bills, and "education bills," which are 100 percent unconstitutional.

Do not think our government will hesitate to carry out Socialist undertakings in the United States, and they won't need foreign troops to carry out these plans. Europe and the United States are being decimated by drugs, sex, rock music and hedonism. We are losing our cultural heritage, so despised by Aurellio Peccei. The United States hierarchy has been the biggest troublemaker in the world. Since the close of WWII, we have been responsible for destabilizing countries and destroying their national character and identity. Look at South Africa, Zimbabwe (formerly Rhodesia), South Korea, the Philippines, Nicaragua, Panama, Yugoslavia and Iraq to name but a few countries that have been betrayed by the United States.

CHAPTER 6

FOREIGN POLICY DECISIONS

We, the People, are being shut out of government; we are being ignored and our fate is in the hands of gun grabbers and those who have no regard for the Constitution-abortionists-baby— murderers, Socialist power grabbers and all manner of modern day carpetbaggers. The common denominator, easy to trace through all ancient and modern occult theocracies, is blood lust.

Looking back in history, we see that the pages of history books are stained with the blood of the martyrs of Christianity; of decent republican representative governments. These actual holocausts are barely remembered, let alone memorialized. The Club of Rome has an American chapter, which grows stronger each year. Here follows a list of its members:

> William Whipsinger. International Association of Machinists

> Sir Peter Vickers Hall. Behind-the-scenes controller of the Heritage Foundation

> Stuart Butler. *Heritage Foundation*

> Steven Hessler. Heritage Foundation

- Lane Kirkland. *AFL CIO chief executive*
- Irwin Suall. M16 and ADL operative
- Roy Maras Cohn. Former Counsel to the late Sen. Joe McCarthy
- Henry Kissinger. Needs no introduction
- Richard Falck. Princeton University (selected by the COR to wage war on South Africa, Iran and South Korea)
- Douglas Frazier. United Auto Workers Union
- Max Fisher. United Brands Fruit Company
- Averill Harriman. Doyen of the Democrat Party, Socialist confidant of the Rockefeller family
- Jean Kirkpatrick. Former U.S. Ambassador to the U.N.
- Elmo Zumwalt. Admiral, U.S. Navy
- Michaeel Novak. American Enterprise Institute
- Cyrus Vance. Former secretary of state
- April Glaspie. Former Ambassador to Iraq
- Milton Friedman. Economist
- Paul Volcker. Federal Reserve banks
- Gerald Ford. Former President
- Charles Percy. Former U.S. Senator
- Raymond Matthius. Former U.S. Senator
- Michael Harrington. Member of Fabian Society
- Samuel Huntington. Chief planner destroying nations targeted by the COR

> ➤ Claiborne Pell. U.S. Senator
> ➤ Patrick Leahy. U.S. Senator

This is by no means a complete list of the COR's members of the American chapter. Few people have the full list. The Club of Rome is an important international foreign policy arm of the Committee of 300.

It is the executor and overseer of the Committee's foreign policy decisions. The COR gets financial backing from the German Marshall Fund, which has nothing whatever to do with Germany, the name chosen with the intent to dissemble. German Marshall Fund members include, but are not limited, to the following:

> ➤ Milton Katz. Ford Foundation
> ➤ David Rockefeller. Chase Manhattan Bank
> ➤ Russell Train. President of the World Wildlife Fund, Aspen Institute
> ➤ James A. Perkins. Carnegie Corp., a branch of Carnegie Trust of the U.K. and Society of Friends (Quakers)
> ➤ Paul G. Hoffman. Designer, Morgenthau Plan, New York Life Insurance Co.
> ➤ Irving Bluestone. United Auto Workers Exec Board
> ➤ Elizabeth Midgeley. CBS producer
> ➤ B. R. Gifford. Russell Sage Foundation
> ➤ Willy Brandt. Former President, Socialist International
> ➤ Douglas Dillon. Former U.S. Treasury Sec.

> ➤ John J. McCloy. Harvard University, overseer of the Morgenthau Plan
> ➤ Derek C. Bok. Harvard University
> ➤ John B. Cannon. Harvard University

A short summary follows of the objectives of the German Marshall Fund sponsors of the COR meetings in Washington,

D.C. It is a strong supporter of Socialism around the world. Its core leaders are drawn from the old Black Nobility and European aristocracy. Their political aims are to introduce all of the worst features of autocracy, theocracy and occult theocracy into government.

The destruction of national identity and sovereignty of nations is one of its top goals. There are literally hundreds of their agents in government in the United States at local, State and Federal levels.

We have only to examine the record of scores of members of the House to see just how far the German Marshall Fund has progressed in the overall plan to socialize the United States. People ask me, "Why are you bothered by Socialism?"

The answer is; because Socialism is the most dangerous of the "isms" faced by Western civilization. It is in essence, creeping Communism.

CHAPTER 7

WHAT IS SOCIALISM?

As one of the leaders of Fabian Socialism once said:

> *"Socialism has nowhere to go, but to Communism and Communism is merely Socialism in a hurry."*

The American people will not accept outright Communism; hence it is necessary to feed the unsuspecting masses doses of Socialism until the Communizing process has been completed.

In the case of the COR, they utilized hard cores Socialists like the late Willy Brandt, the former German Socialist President, and John J. McCloy, who were inner-sanctum members of the Morgenthau Group.

McCloy was the post-WWII "high commissioner" of a defeated Germany and lobbied hard to turn it into a pastoral non- industrialized nation.

In this he was greatly aided by Leslie Gelb and Jimmy Carter's Secretary of State Cyrus Vance, both deeply committed Socialists. Gelb and Vance worked tirelessly to disadvantage the United States during the protracted SALT treaty talks.

The dominant inner-group of the Morgenthau planning commission who are members of the German Marshal Fund, include the following:

> Averill Harriman, Brown Bros., Harriman, Wall Street bankers

Harriman was the key U.S. official in the efforts to get the Soviets to join the One World Government, but Stalin's opposition and mistrust of the New World Order run by the United States remained strong and he refused.

> Thomas L. Hughes

Partner in Brown Bros. Harriman. Designer of Morgenthau Plan.

> Robert Abercrombie Lovett

A partner in Brown Bros. Harriman and a designer of the Morgenthau plan.

> Prince Bernhard of the Netherlands

A Royal Dutch Shell Executive (one of the major companies of the Committee of 300 and founder of the Bilderberg Group).

> Katherine Meyer Graham (now deceased)

Doyen of the established press, was a member of the Meyer family and friend of Bernard Baruch and President Wilson. Her father is said to have duplicated WWI bonds and to have kept the millions of dollars generated by the fake bonds. He was never prosecuted.

Graham's husband died in very suspicious circumstances.

Intelligence sources say they believe he was murdered and that his wife had a hand in it—but nothing was ever proved. The Meyer family controlled the huge Lazard Freres investment bank.

> John J. McCloy

The controller of multiple Committees of 300 companies attached to European royalty to whom he acts as financial adviser.

> Professor Samuel Huntington

An ardent Zionist-Socialist involved in the downfall of most of the right-wing governments targeted by the Committee of 300 in the post WWII-era.

> Joseph Rettinger

The Jesuit-Socialist responsible for recruiting Bilderberg members and introducing them to the Harriman group, once worked for Winston Churchill. Rettinger is believed to be the man who recruited Clinton as a possible future Socialist leader and then turned him over to Pamela Harriman for grooming for high office. Rettinger's plan was to make a central European Jesuit state out of Poland, Hungary and Austria, but the post-WWII plan was not approved by the Committee of 300.

Most of the Black Nobility and European royalty are connected through marriage to Britain's oligarchical families going back to Robert Bruce, who founded the Scottish Rite of Freemasonry. Take Lovet for instance. He is a member of the European Union closely allied with

McCloy.

Both men were inner-circle friends of the Auchincloss and Astor families who have close relations with British, Dutch, Danish and Spanish "nobility." Also working with the group were the Radziwills and Zbignew Brzezinski, Carter's national security advisor. All are servants of the Committee of 300. In the Royal Dutch Shell grouping there was Sir Bazil Zaharoff, the former president of Vickers Arms Company, the British arms manufacturing company that made billions out of supplying munitions for the Bolshevik Revolution, WWI and WWII. The family of Sir Peter Vickers Hall, (behind the scenes controller of the Heritage Foundation in Washington D.C.), were the inheritors of this vast fortune. The control figures of the American chapter of the COR are:

> Jean Kirkpatrick,

> Eugene Rostow,

> Irwin Suall,

> Michael Novack,

> Lane Kirkland,

> Albert Chaitkin,

> Jeremy Rifkin,

> Douglas Frazier,

> Marcus Raskin,

> William Kunsler.

These worthies need no introduction. They are Socialist leaders of great importance in the war to socialize the United States. Co- workers in the struggle to overturn the republican form of government enjoyed by the United States are the following:

- ➢ Gar Apelrovich,
- ➢ Ben Watenburg,
- ➢ Irving Bluestone,
- ➢ Nat Weinberg,
- ➢ Sol Chaikan,
- ➢ Jay Lovestone,
- ➢ Mary Fine,
- ➢ Jacob Shankman,
- ➢ Ron Dellums,
- ➢ George McGovern,
- ➢ Richard Bonnett,
- ➢ Barry Commoner,
- ➢ Noam Chomsky,
- ➢ Robert Moss,
- ➢ David McReynolds,
- ➢ Frederik von Hayek,
- ➢ Sidney Hook,
- ➢ Seymour Martin Lipsit,
- ➢ Ralph Widner.

The above-named were affiliated with various Socialist organizations like the AFL-CIO International Affairs Department, the Cambridge Institute for Contemporary Studies, the Institute of Policy Studies, the Auto Workers

Union and the International Ladies Garment Workers Union with its long ties to Fabian Socialism.

Von Hayek is dearly beloved by conservatives as their economist of choice. Senators George McGovern and Ron Dellums both served in the United States Congress.

Some of the Socialist publications put out by the abovementioned are:

> The New Republic—Richard Stuart and Morton Condrake

> The Nation—Nat Hentoff, Marcus Raskin, Norman Benorn, Richard Faulk, Andrew Kopkind

> Dissent - Irving Hall, Michael Harrington Commentary — Carl Girshman

> The Working Paper for a New Society—Marcus Raskin. Noam Chomsky, Gar Apelrovich, Andrew Kopkind, James Ridgway

> Enquiry—Nat Hentoff

> WIN— Noam Chomsky

With so many levels in its serried ranks, it might be useful to view the Club of Rome as a giant Socialist think-tank. How the COR got started is very interesting.

When the Club of Rome needed to coordinate some of the aspects of its program for the New World Order, it sent Aurellio Peccei to England for training at the Tavistock Institute of Human Relations, the mother of all brainwashing institutions in the world.

At the time, Peccei was the most senior executive of the Fiat Motor Company, a giant multi-conglomerate of the Committee of 300 through its Black Nobility members, the aristocratic Agnelli family, the same family who rejected Pamela Harriman as the wife of one of the Agnelli sons.

Pamela went on to marry Averill Harriman, a senior 300 Statesman and U.S. foreign policy specialist, a true "insider."

THE CLUB OF ROME

CHAPTER 8

NATO AND THE CLUB OF ROME

Tavistock was under the direction and control of Major General John Rawlings Reese, who had the assistance of Lord Bertrand Russell, the Huxley brothers, Kurt Lewin and Eric Trist as his new science-scientist specialists.

Regular subscribers to *World In Review* will know that all manner of evils darkness, chaos and confusion invaded the United States with the arrival of Tavistock missionaries. Aldous Huxley and Bertrand Russell, who were prominent members of the cult of Isis-Osiris.

After being stripped of what few human qualities he had started with, Tavistock certified Peccei as "qualified" and dispatched him to the headquarters of the North Atlantic Treaty Organization (NATO.)

This Committee of 300 organization was structured primarily as a political body, and secondarily—as a military defense pact group for Europe against the dangers presented by the USSR. At NATO, Peccei recruited top members to follow him in forming the Club of Rome. Attached to COR were other NATO and various political left-wing leaders, who formed the Bilderberg Group, the Socialist recruiting and training arm of the Committee of 300.

What were the aims and objectives of the COR? Essentially, they followed the Communist Manifesto of 1848, and were Socialist in character and origin, motivated by dark spiritual forces in play in Gnosticism, Chaldean Black Magic, Rosicrucianism, the Cults of Isis-Osiris and Dionysus, Demonism, Occult Theocracy, Luciferianism, Freemasonry and the like. The overthrow of Western Christian civilization was paramount to COR activity.

The destruction of national sovereignty and nationalism of all nations and with it, the destruction of billions of human beings "surplus to requirements" was also high on the COR's agenda. Peccei believed that nation-states, individual liberty, religion, and freedom of expression had to be ground to dust under the boot of the New World Order-One World Government, through COR was established to do in the shortest as possible time. COR think-tanks had the task of bringing together under one umbrella organization, the many Socialist organizations already striving to end Western Christian civilization.

Japan cannot be left out of COR-Committee of 300 plans. Japan is also an industrial nation, a highly nationalistic homogenous people; the kind of society much hated by the would-be rulers of the New World Order. Therefore, Japan, although not Western or Christian, presented a problem to the COR planners.

Using David Rockefeller's Japan Society and Suntory Foundation, the plan was to undermine Japan's most successful use of the American economic system—a legacy left to it by General Douglas MacArthur, by applying indirect means. "Indirect means" meant indoctrinating Japan with Socialist ideals, so-called "cultural changes" according to the blueprint, the "Age of Aquarius-New

Age." Japan's institutions and traditions were to be slowly but surely undermined in the manner and by method adopted against the United States.

The COR fanatics who waged war on America to "change its public image" were unleashed against Japan. Daniel Bell of Tavistock and Daniel Yankelovich, the number 1 American "image makers" were called in to divert, at least on a temporary basis, and wage their war against Japan's industrial base. Those of you, who have followed my work since I began in 1970, will know that the interfacing of British Intelligence MI6 and David Sarnoff of the Radio Corporation of America (RCA) led to British agents being placed in key positions inside the CIA and the FBI's Division Five—its counterintelligence arm. Yankelovich, of the firm Yankelovich, Skelly and White was co-opted by MI6 to wage a ceaseless war on the American people.

Yankelovich, an anti-Christian Socialist who had been in the vanguard of the onslaught against an unsuspecting American people for two decades was now ordered by the COR to concentrate his resources on attacks against heavy industry in Japan, what they called, "belching smoke stacks." Light industry was to be praised and commended.

The hope was that the postindustrial zero-growth collapse of the United States and Volcker's credit crunch tactics could be repeated against Japan. In a postindustrial society, according to the COR, close to 50 million Americans were to be deprived of their jobs and be left permanently jobless, and many millions more, would be underemployed. This, the COR reckoned, would lead to social and moral decay, making the nation an easy victim for the New World Order-One World Government takeover. The collapse of the American middle class would have a profound effect on

Japan's exports to the United States.

Like the American people, who have never been made aware of the war raging against them since 1946, COR-planners hoped to catch the Japanese nation off-guard. Peter Berger of the infamous Council on Foreign Relations (CFR)—the upper-level, parallel government of the United States under the Committee of 300, and the so-called anthropologist, Herbert Passon—the man who stepped into the shoes of the late, unlamented Margaret Mead, happily took up their new challenge. As a result, a flood of "New Age" literature hit the Japanese market, purporting to show just how far industry in Japan had driven the average Japanese away from national, traditional values.

Made for television movies of street gangs of "Rock and Roll" youths were made popular with being care taken not to disclose that this aberration came from the same source that gave us the Beatles, Mick Jagger, Keith Richard and all manner of decadent, depraved amoral reprobates are the creation of the Tavistock Institute under the aegis of the COR. Jagger and Richards were often honored by European royalty. The image thus created is that such degeneracy is the consequence of the industrialization of the United States.

Unless there is a concerted effort made to prevent it, Japan is slated to undergo the same moral decline, or at least equal in severity to that which was experienced by the United States of the "Beatles-Jagger-Rolling Stones" era roughly from the 1960s to the 1980s. Incidentally, Jagger and Richards belong to the occult club established by Luciferian Alestair Crowley ~ the Isis-Osiris Order of the Golden Dawn. The principal objective of Isis-Osiris is the moral destruction of the youth of the West through unlimited drugs abuse, "free sex," homosexuality and lesbianism.

The "music" provided by degenerates like Jagger and some later rock band leaders, set the tone for the lowering of inhibitions, making the youth of the nations more easily to induct into these evil practices. The problem facing the COR is now to deal with the backlash that will surely come when unemployment as in Japan reaches U.S. levels. The Japanese are unlikely to meekly submit and accept unemployment's their American counterparts have already done.

Japan is a tough country to crack, but by feeding its poison slowly, in measured doses, the COR hopes to achieve a revolution in Japan, which will not arouse the populace—in other words, the American model is to be followed in the coming attack on Japan. In the United States, the Club of Rome's "Aquarian Conspiracy" has enjoyed stunning success. A summarized version of COR's Willis Harmon's paper on the subject is all that we need to understand what is going on:

Images and fundamental conception of human nature and potentialities can have enormous power in shaping the values and actions in a society. He (that is Harmon and the COR) have attempted to study this by:

> Illuminati ways.

> Explore with respect to contemporary society problems, the deficiencies of currently held images of mankind, and to identify needed characteristics of future images.

> Identify high-level activities that could facilitate the emergence of a *New Image* (emphasis added)

and new policies approaches to the resolution of key problems in society.

We use the image of man or man in the universe to refer to the set of assumptions held about the human being's origin, nature, abilities and characteristics, relationship with others and place in the universe. A coherent image might be held by any individual or group or political system, a church or civilization. Most societies have an image of man, which defines his social nature. For example, an image of man is thus a gestalt perception of human kind, both individual and collective in relation to self the society and the cosmos.

This is unadulterated nonsense, occult hocus-pocus designed to deceive the unwary. For most, assumptions about the nature of human beings are held subconsciously. But to continue with Harmon's attempt to brainwash us:

Only when these hidden assumptions are recognized and brought into awareness is an image of man constructed, the image can be carefully examined with perspective retained and discarded or changed (emphasis added.) Many of our present images appear to have become dangerously obsolescent. An image may be appropriate to one phase in the development of a society, but once that stage is accomplished, the use of the image, as a continuing guide to action will likely create more problems than it solves. Science, technology and economics have made possible really significant strides toward achieving such basic human goals as physical safety and security, material comfort and better health.

But many of these successes have brought with them the problem of being too successful. Problems which themselves seem insoluble within the set of social value premises that lead to their emergence. Our highly developed technological system led to vulnerability and breakdown. The interconnected impact of society problems that have emerged now pose a serious threat to our civilization.

In other words, our Western ideals, belief in family, the sanctity of marriage, belief in one's country, national pride, national sovereignty, pride in our religious beliefs, pride of race, our trust in an omnipotent God and our Christian beliefs, are all obsolescent—according to the COR's Harmon.

The illuminist and high priest of the COR believes that "being too successful" springs from being too successful as an industrialized nation with full employment and a people enjoying a decent standard of living.

CHAPTER 9

A RETURN TO THE DARK AGES

Harmon meant that Americans, thanks to an industry-based society, were enjoying too much freedom and this led to a position, where there are just too many people, who must, therefore, be corralled and culled, so that the COR can curb industrial growth, and therefore population growth. The truth is that Christian Western civilization does pose a threat—not to civilization—but to the occult theocracy future planed for the world by the Committee of 300.

What Harmon advocates is a return to the Dark Ages, a New Dark Age, under a one World Government dictatorship.

Harmon, the high priest of the COR, laid out a scenario that is in direct contradiction with God's law, which says that we must be fruitful, and multiply and subdue the Earth, not for the benefit of the COR and the Committee of 300, but for the freedom of our people in the United States and others who choose to respect their national identities.

The Luciferians served by Harmon, the members of the Cult of Dionysus, the "Olympians"—they say, "No, we were placed here to rule the Earth and we alone shall enjoy its benefits." High priest Harmon concludes as follows:

We must change the industrial technological image of man— fast. Our analyses of the nature of contemporary society problems leads to the conclusion that the images of many that dominated the last two centuries will he inadequate for the postindustrial era. The image of man appropriate to that new world (not new—the concept, a Satanic one, is four thousand years old) must be sought, synthesized and then wired into mankind's brains.

The image that emerged from the Italian Renaissance, the economic man, individualist, materialist, seeking objective knowledge, this is inappropriate and must be discarded. The industrial state at this point has immense drive but no direction, marvelous capacity to get there, but no idea where it is going. Somehow the breakdown of the old images has been seen to lead more to despair rather than to a search for a new image. Despite the pessimism implied by a lagging dominant image, there are numerous indications that a new anticipatory image of mankind may be emerging.

What this mumbo-jumbo really means—what Harmon was really saying—was that industrialized societies, like the United States and Japan must be destroyed as industrialized society has become unmanageable. With the destruction of industry, Harmon postulated, would come the destruction of all of our basic morals, our basic beliefs in God and country, our Christian-based culture, which will lead swiftly to the return to the world of an **occult theocracy** of the new dark ages COR high-priest Harmon said:

… nineteen images of man dominate various epochs, and from each he extracts such features he believes useful for replacing the industrial technological image, programs the COR and the Committee hope to emulate and which will turn the people of the world—those that are left as mindless slaves after the culling of Global 2000 has

occurred, in a New Dark Age—the so-called New World Order.

According to the Harmon plan, mankind is to be identified as part of the animal kingdom. Harmon says that the ruling elite are ordained in the postindustrial image and the Old Testament image of man having dominion over all of nature must be dropped, as it is dangerous.

The Zoroastrian image rather, is favored. The Indian Asian system of yoga is preferable to Christianity—this according to Harmon, as this will bring about the needed "self realization." This euphemism is simply a device used by Harmon to indicate that Christianity must be replaced by occult beliefs such as were practiced by the members of Isis-Osiris and the Cult of Dionysus. The Christian image of mankind must be replaced, this according to high priest Harmon. Man must stop thinking that he needs God. It is high time for man to believe that he is in control of his destiny and can stand on his own feet.

What is lacking in our Christian churches today is the knowledge and understanding of the occult and the occult—ridden secret societies that are everywhere to be found. Our Christian teachers and readers need to become versed in the field of religious theocracies, and where they are leading the Church of Christ.

Rather than discard the beauty and purity of the Renaissance, we need to cling to it all the harder and protect its priceless heritage. Here is an outline of some of the steps advocated by Harmon, in order to make the COR's plans for a New World Order work:

➤ Youth involvement in the political processes.

> Women's liberation movements.

> Black consciousness.

> Youth rebellion against "wrongs" in society.

> Greater interest in Social responsibility of business.

> The generation gap.

> Induced bias against industry and technology in the youth.

> Experimenting with new family structures (i.e. single parent, homosexual "couples" and lesbian "households.")

> Conservative ecology groups must be formed.

> Interest in Eastern religions to be diligently applied in schools and universities.

These points in the Harmon Manifesto can almost be overlaid on the Communist Manifesto of 1848. There are minor differences in style rather than substance, but the basic premise that the world must become a Socialist state that will advance to Communism is a common thread found in both documents. The underlying, hidden theme is the same as the Communist—Bolsheviks taught: "Get in our way at your peril. Terror tactics are our tactics, and we will use them without fear or favor. We will eliminate you if you oppose us." As I said earlier, the New Age ideal as set forth by Harmon is thousands of years old. The Druids burned people in wicker baskets as sacrifices to their gods and their women priestesses let the blood of their victims flow into buckets.

The French Revolution took the lives of hundreds of thousands of innocent victims, as did the Bolshevik

Revolution. The Communists were proud of the way they tortured and murdered millions of Christians. What makes us think that the COR, an **occult theocracy** will not do likewise when it gets the chance? These are the murderous, spiritually dead people we are dealing with, the people described by Christ as the rulers of darkness, the wicked in high places, and it is high time that every one of us, whether Japanese or American, awoke to the dangers facing civilization.

When this attack on God and mankind was recorded by Harmon in 1974, the fourteen principles behind Harmon were careful not to reveal any direct involvement by the various institutions they intended using to manufacture, set up and them bring to the forefront as a counterculture battering ram. Drunk with power and anticipating a docile American public that would not react, Harmon decided to use Marilyn Ferguson as a front, to let the cat out of the bag.

Harmon chose Marilyn Ferguson, a totally unknown untalented women who shot to fame as the alleged author of "The Aquarian Conspiracy," a translation into a book of fiction, but Harmon did not tell the public that Ferguson and all participants were merely kept hirelings of the COR, and it was the COR that gave life to the *Aquarian Conspiracy*.

This new version of an age-old conspiracy first saw the light of day in 1960 and continued to grow like a cancer on the body— politic throughout 1968, spreading the post-industrial message of a counter-culture based upon occult secret societies, whose names are legion.

The founders have already been named. Its official organs were Tavistock Institute, the Institute of Social Relations and Stanford Research Center, where applied social psychiatry played a pivotal role in forming and guiding NATO to adopt the long-term strategy of the COR, which was dubbed by the establishment as the Aquarian-New Age movement.

Many people have written to me during the course of my career, asking me why I haven't written about the "New World Order." Well, I have been writing these subjects and many more since 1969. The trouble was that people didn't listen to someone as unknown as I was, then. But when some crackpot like Marilyn Ferguson, backed the power of the Rockefeller Foundation came along with the exact same thing I had been warning of, they asked, "Where were you; why didn't you tell us this?"

The truth is I did draw the attention of those who were subscribers to my work, to the New Age of Aquarius, the Club of Rome and the Committee of 300, long before these names reached the attention of others—ten-fifteen years before, to be precise.

In retrospect, my reports were years before their time, long before these things were known to any other rightwing writers in America.

One of the earlier onslaughts against the United States began with the Cuban missile crisis, when John F. Kennedy rejected the advice of the Tavistock Institute, the CFR, Rand Institute and Stanford. That made Kennedy a man marked for elimination. His murder, still veiled in swathes of conflicting reports is a major insult to the American people. I told what I know of the perpetrators of this most heinous crime in my book "The Committee of 300," revised, updated and published in January 2007.

Kennedy took a "flexible response" defense strategy, which was not based on psychological warfare put out by NATO's political wing through Civil Defense planners. But Kennedy opted to scale down civil defense and pressed forward instead with a massive new space program for the technological upgrading of American industry. By so doing, Kennedy signed his death warrant. Observe the power of the forces of the One World-New World Order theocracy. They had no hesitation in murdering the President of the United States in November of 1963.

Early in 1963, a certain assassination bureau, whose name I am not at liberty to disclose, signed a contract with the Tavistock Institute of Human Relations. Note the misuse of the words, "human relations." The contract was farmed out to several U.S. subsidiaries of Tavistock, notably, Stanford Research, the Institute of Social Relations and the Rand Corporation.

Tavistock then made public the results of the "scientific studies" conducted by these think tanks and then fed the information to NATO's political wing.

Those of you who place your hopes in NATO better get wise to what is going on. NATO is a creature of the COR, and does the bidding of that organized servant—body of the Committee of 300.

CHAPTER 10

SECRET SOCIETIES RULE FROM BEHIND THE SCENES

Following this development, in 1966, Dr. Anatol Rappaport, editor-in-chief of Tavistock's *Human Relations Magazine*, reported that NASA's space program was redundant, and that the United States was fiddling around in space programs when it should have been spending the money on "human quality" studies.

It was anticipated that the Human Relations Magazine report would turn public opinion in the United States against space programs. After the murder of Kennedy, it seemed for a while, as if our space program would be abandoned, then came the stunning election victory of Ronald Reagan in November, which led to the unprecedented meeting of high-level executives of the COR in Washington in November of 1980.

As I often indicated in my lectures and writings since 1969, the world is run by very different people from those we see up front, an observation first made famous by Lord Beaconsfield (Disraeli). We are from time to time given ample warning of the truth of this observation, but in a veiled manner. It seems that the would-be rulers of the One World Government are sometimes quite unable to contain themselves when they pull off a big victory.

An example of what I mean was provided by Colonel Mandel House, the controller of Presidents Wilson and Roosevelt. House wrote a book, *Phillip Drew: Administrator,* supposedly fiction, but in reality a detailed account of how the secret government of the United States was to be sold into slavery in a One World Government-New World Order.

Disraeli, the legendary British Prime Minister and great parliamentarian protege of the Rothschilds, gave an account of the workings of the secret government of Britain entitled, *Conningsby,* which gave notice that secret groups controlling the British and United States Governments intended to rule the world. Secret societies have been and remain the nemesis of the free world. As long as we have such diverse large numbers of secret societies flourishing in our midst, we're not free men. No amount of flag-waving and banging the big drum of patriotism on the 4th of July can change this stark truth.

The secret societies have leaders that rule the world from behind the scenes, and, if we are to understand current events in politics and economics, then we better have a good knowledge of secret societies.

The Club of Rome (COR) is but an extension, an ongoing alliance of the ancient Black Nobility families of Europe, dominated by occult beliefs and practices dating back for thousands of years. The ancient rite of Mizraim of Egypt, (before the arrival of the sons of Noah), Syria, Babylon and Persia were transported to Europe by the Venetian and British oligarchists.

The Bogomils, the Catharis—these are the types of

THE CLUB OF ROME

"religious beliefs" that brought in their wake an assault on Christian views and Western principles. The Eastern love of intrigue was transplanted in the West, with results so far reaching that they beggar description, often beyond the scope of our imagination.

The damage these secret societies do is awesome. For instance, we know that the Crimean War was started on a whim of Freemasonry, with WWI and WWII following much along the same lines. We can never know just how far the dark, secret forces of secret societies in our midst influence current events.

The Boer War, probably the most important war of the 20th century, because it pitted secret societies and their mystery religions against a freedom-loving Christian Nation of patriotic people, aggressors whose intent was to rob the Boers of their newly discovered gold. One of the most powerful men in British politics during that unseemly period in the history of Great Britain was Lord Palmerston, who belonged to many secret societies, and whose leadership of the Parliament was influenced by Freemasonry. Palmerston himself admitted to this being true.

Thus it behooves We, the People, to wake up to the fact that we are in contention with spiritually wicked men in high places. We are not up against mere physical entities. The unseen force is stronger than the seen force. These forces are in control of the United States and we see it in the fact that more than 75 percent of the Democrat members of the House and Senate are out—and— out Socialists.

Harlan Cleveland

JOHN COLEMAN

Perhaps the best-known member of the USACOR is Harlan Cleveland, former U.S. ambassador to NATO during the 1960s and a former vice chairman of the Atlantic Council, NATO'S main presence in the United States.

Cleveland headed the Princeton, New Jersey office of the Aspen Institute for Humanistic Studies, the branch office in America of the Tavistock Institute of Human Relations. Aspen is supposedly a "think tank" dedicated to environmentalist issues, but this is merely a fig leaf, a smoke screen to cover its real activities—making war on United States industry and agriculture.

William Watts

A member of the Atlantic Council and a director of Tomack Associates, the front for circulating COR's *Limits of Growth* 1972–1973 study purporting to show how industry and "excess agricultural development" is ruining the ecology. Watts is in charge of distributing Aspen's disguised version of the old Thomas Malthus theory of zero growth, which actually has its origins in the ancient cult of Dionysus.

George McGee

McGee, a member of the Atlantic Council, is a former Undersecretary of State for the political affairs wing of NATO and a former U.S. ambassador to Turkey. Later he served as U.S. ambassador to Bonn, Germany.

Claiborne K. Pell

Pell was the United States Senator from Rhode Island and a

former U.S. parliamentary representative to the Atlantic Council. Pell is strong advocate of the COR's policy that NATO forces should oversee enforcement of environmental standards around the world. Pell strongly supports deindustrialization of all nations, including the United States. He has often expressed sympathy with Russell's theory about "excess population" being culled. Pell served with Cyrus Vance in drafting the terms of the Global 2000 Report. Pell cooperates with Cyrus Vance and NATO Secretary-General Joseph Lunz, and often attends Bilderberg meetings.

Donald Lesh

A former employee of Tomack Associates, Lesh is executive director of USACOR. He also served at one time on the National Security Agency (NSA) and helped Kissinger put together the European apparatus of the NSA, in which endeavor he worked with Helmut Sonenfelt, who has been tied to Kissinger like a Siamese twin since the discovery of the Bamberg Files. William Highland, touted as a Soviet specialist also worked for NSA's European office.

Sol Linowitz

Better known for drafting the fraudulent unconstitutional Panama Canal Treaty, Linowitz became a Carter confidant, and he enjoyed high standing in the Committee of 300's Rank Xerox Corporation and is a member of the Committee of 300.

J. Walter Lew

Levy is the in-house oil analyst for the New York Council
on Foreign Relations (CFR) and a director of the Atlantic
Council and a member of the Bilderberg group. Levy drew
up the program for the Brandt Commission of international
Socialist policy makers. While Brandt is nearly always
inebriated, he is, nevertheless, one of the most dangerous
Socialists on the contemporary scene today.

Joseph Slater

Slater is a director of Aspen Institute, the Socialist
headquarters for the Committee of 300 in the United States.
He was formerly a U.S. ambassador to NATO. These are
some of the chief players in a nest of seditionists who are
located in the United States. Their chief function is to speed
up the Post Industrial Zero Growth plan developed by the
COR and to turn the former northeastern industrial cities
into slave labor entities under the title of "enterprise zones."
A target was President Reagan's SDI program, which
would forever put an end to Kissinger and Robert
McNamara's MAD strategy. NATO is deployed to bring
together all aspects of the anti-American program.

CHAPTER 11

NASA AND THE CLUB OF ROME

An example of this was U.S. participation in the Malvinas (Falklands) War, when United States provided support facilities that made it possible for British forces to defeat Argentina, which had to be laid low, because of its excellent nuclear power plant export program.

One of the American Club of Rome's main achievements to date was to remove the space program from the military and give it to NASA, a civilian body. Former President Eisenhower was more than happy to comply with the instructions he received from London to implement the change.

But the move may have backfired. In May of 1967, a profiling study of NASA undertaken by the Tavistock Institute of Human Relations found that NASA had become a major employer of industrial and science personnel, the exact opposite of the de- industrializing plans of COR. The Tavistock report set alarm bells ringing in the offices of the seditionists and traitors, from Colorado to Washington to New York.

Their response was a "select committee" under the direction of NATO Robert Strauss Haptfz, U.S. ambassador to

NATO. The job of the committee was to immediately institute damage control measures, which it was hoped would cripple NASA. A meeting was called to discuss what was called, "transatlantic technological imbalance and collaboration." The meeting was held in Deauville, France and was attended by Aurellio Peccei and Zbigniew Brzezinski.

The gathering of seditionists and enemies of the people of the United States was conveniently overlooked by the media, the very same media that would later strive mightily—and succeed—in removing President Nixon from the White House.

It was at this meeting that Brzezinski obtained inspiration for his book, *Between Two Ages: The Technotronic Era,* which I quoted in length in my book, *The Committee of 300.*

In this book, Brzezinski lays out the ideal of a Socialist New World Order, based on Orwellian concepts; a world run by an intellectual elite and a super-culture based on a network of electronic communications, in a concept of regionalism with symbolic national sovereignty.

The Deauville conference concluded that there must be a convergence of ideals between the United States and the USSR (an idea totally rejected by Stalin who was a real thorn in the side of the Committee of 300).

The "convergence" would produce a One World Government to run global affairs on a true basis of crisis management and global planning. It will be recalled that this Rockefeller suggestion was scorned by Stalin and it was his refusal to join the New World Order that led to the

Korean War.

Even the twisted, censored, heavily laced with inaccuracies history of WWII written by paid Rockefeller writers shows that the United States has never fought Communism. How could it, when the elite of the Wilson era and the Wall Street bankers were the very ones who placed Lenin and Trotsky in power in collusion with Lord Alfred Milner and the City of London bankers?

The Second World War was a contrived situation. Hitler was set up by the Wall Street and City of London bankers ostensibly to corral Stalin and bring him to heel, after he began rejecting the overtures to establish "joint world rule."

Stalin did not trust what he called, "the Washington cosmopolitans." Hitler was destroyed because he turned against his controllers, who then in their dialectical manner, backed Stalin to the hilt in what they perceived to be the lesser danger of the two. Unable to control Hitler, the international bankers had to destroy him.

The net outcome of WWII was the emergence of a stronger, more formidable Communist system, able to spread its tentacles over the globe. The Soviet Union went from a regional power, to a global power.

WWII cost millions of lives and billions of dollars, and it was all because of the shocking misuse of resources by men with grandiose plans to rule the world and I am not talking about Hitler and Stalin. I am talking about the CFR, the RIIA, the Club of Rome and the Committee of 300. If anyone can give me a list of the alleged benefits accrued from WWII or explain the "freedoms" that it has brought to the people of America, or Europe, I would like to hear from them.

As far as I can see, the world is a thousand times worse off now than it was in 1939. Socialism has taken hold of the United States as a consequence of WWII. Our industries have been destroyed; millions of workers have lost their jobs. We can't blame Hitler (or Stalin) for this contrived state of affairs. Peccei put it in prospective when he said:

> ... *Since the millennium was approached in Christendom, in large, masses of people are really in suspense about impending events of things unknown which could change their collective fate entirely. Man does not know how to be a truly modern man.*

What Peccei was telling us is that the cultists, the esoterics, the New Agers—they know what is good for us, and that we had better conform to the dictates of the New World Order or be destroyed.

We must learn to live with and behave in the framework of the COR's *Limits of Growth* pattern, which includes a limit on what religions we can follow. We must learn to live within the constraints on our economy imposed by the COR and not rebel against the new monetary order.

We must also accept the idea that we are expendable. Peccei says that "man invented the story of the bad dragon, but if ever there was a bad dragon on earth, it is man himself."

Peccei then gives the whole game plan away:

> *Since man opened the Pandora's box of new technology, he has suffered uncontrollable human proliferation; the*

mania for growth, the energy crisis, actual potential scarcities, degradation of the environment, nuclear folly, and countless other afflictions.

CHAPTER 12

THE MESS OF THE MONEY SYSTEMS

I n these few words are found the entire plans for mankind mapped out by the COR for the Committee of 300. This answers in a nutshell, the most often asked question: *"Why would they want to do these things?"* Here we have an esoterist of the worst degree telling the people that the COR speaking on behalf of its masters of the Committee of 300 knows what is best for the entire world.

It was not long after his speech that Peccei adopted the "World Dynamics" model, constructed for the Committee of 300 by Jay Forrester and Dennis Meadows, which is a global planning model supposedly to demonstrate the unsustainability of complex systems to show that smaller-in-scale structures should predominate in the world economy. To this end, of course, the Meadows-Forrester report based its ideas exclusively on the negative, restrictive economic studies done by Malthus and Adam Smith, the British East India economist, who formulated Britain's "free trade" policy.

The Forrestor Meadows mythical economy ignores the ingenuity of man, who will find an endless supply of new minerals and or resources of which we as yet have no knowledge. Actually, what is depleting our resources is paper money, if we can call anything paper, "money."

The money system of the United States is a gigantic mess thanks to the meddling of those in the oligarchical hierarchy, whose intention is to make slaves of us all.

Only un-backed paper money is doing damage to the natural resources of the globe, and by un-backed, I mean U.S. dollars are not backed by silver and gold as called for by the Constitution of the United States of America. In fact there is no lawful money in the United States at this time, nor has there been since the advent of the Federal Reserve Act.

It is no wonder that we are in such a financial mess, when a private consortium (The Federal Reserve Bank) was permitted to take charge of our money and use it in whatever manner it deemed fit, without the people to whom it belongs having the slightest control over it.

An economy based on gold and silver will renew and recycle natural resources. In nuclear fission, a fission-based society would open new windows of opportunity. Yet Meadows and Forrestor ignored the magic of the fusion torch. How the COR could ignore new technologies is easily explained. Quite simply they did not want them.

New technologies mean new jobs and a more prosperous people. More prosperous people mean an increase in the population of North America, which COR spokesmen say is undesirable and a threat to life on Earth!

The truth of the matter is that we haven't even begun to tap the natural resources of the earth. The whole New Dark Ages, New World Order concept, from Russell to Peccei, to Meadows and Forrestor is fatally flawed and designed to retard industrial growth, jobs, and, finally, a culling of the population of the world.

(NOTE: The United Nations Conference on Population Control held in Cairo in August of 1994, was but an extension of the Global 2000 plan to kill 2.5 billion people by the year 2010.)

Regarding nuclear power, Peccei said:

> *I am more pessimistic and radical than my friends in judging the nuclear solution. I am not in a position to judge or even guess whether this can be made clean, secure and reliable for human society as many scientists and almost the totality of the political class and industry affirm.*

> *I am however ready to argue that what is not reliable, secure and clean enough,* **is human society itself.** *I have devoted many pages to describing its state of disorder, its incapacity to govern itself, to act rational and humanely and to ease the tensions which tear it apart and hence I cannot believe that in its present state it can go nuclear.*

This is almost a carbon copy of what the environmentalist groups are saying about nuclear power, which just happens to be the cheapest, cleanest and safest source of energy available to the world.

It is also a vehicle which would create millions of new, stable, long term steady jobs.

> *I cannot imagine that this same society will be in a condition within a couple of decades to safely host and protect several thousand huge nuclear power stations and to transport across the planet and process even a quarter of the deadly plutonium 239, ten thousands of times greater than what it would take to kill all of us living today.*

For mankind to go nuclear without first being prepared in its entire human system for its reckless and irresponsible behavior is the question; the real problems are not technical or economic, but political, social and cultural.

Those who are today inebriated by just small doses of the nuclear hard drug as I have called it, and are pushing a program to disseminate it in the body of society are in effect condemning their successes to live entirely by it tomorrow.

And why not! Nuclear energy is the greatest discovery the world has ever known. It will set us free. That is why the enemies of mankind, the Club of Rome, are fighting on every front to downgrade nuclear energy to make out that it is such a terrible danger to us. Nuclear energy is safe. Thus far, nobody had been killed by a nuclear generated energy while working in such a power station.

It will give us great freedom, it will revitalize our industrial capacities—it will breathe new life into them and it will give us greater freedom as individuals, because millions more of us will have long term, well paid-jobs. Greater freedom is an anathema to the Club of Rome. The Club of Rome wants less personal freedom, not more of it. That is the bottom line on the issue of nuclear energy.

Peccei went on to dismiss nuclear fission in one sentence and he said:

Its feasibility has yet to be demonstrated, but no future plan can at present be reliably based upon it. There is little probability of energy becoming plentiful, inexpensive and environmentally and socially unobjectionable.

If abundant, cheap, clean energy were available, the

> *prospects of technology intensifying solutions for food and*
> *materials would be very good.*

Now, he stopped short there, but here's the rub: The Club of Rome does not wish us to intensify our technological capabilities and produce more food and produce a better living standard.

It has designed a program called Global 2000, which calls for the death of 2 billion people by the year 2010, although the bottom line figure that I have seen in the report states that the Club of Rome will be satisfied if 400 million people are wiped off the face of the Earth by the year 2010.

Peccei made it quite plain that the new scientific discoveries and new technologies as a means of increasing material progress is not desired by the Club of Rome, who pretends to be the sole arbiter of global planning under NATO.

This, of course, is after they have taken in and subdued a rebellious Russia. And I say again, that what we see in the world today is a disagreement between America and Russia. Peccei used the artificially-created oil embargo of the 1973 Arab-Israeli war, as a warning. He said this brought "many people into alignment with Club of Rome thinking."

It was in effect an entry point for many people to break with former ways of thinking and to take the Club of Rome's advice much more seriously. I have said before that these people sometimes cannot keep their mouths closed. Here you have a man openly admitting that the 1973 Arab-Israeli war was a contrived situation of a phony oil shortage in the world and by so doing, convinced more people that smaller is better and more beautiful and that industrial progress had to be curbed.

The rationale of the Club of Rome, of course, is that proof of these statements as made in the Forrester-Meadows reports, was brought home to many people by the 1973 oil embargo. During the period 1973-74, the Club of Rome's influence over the policies of many governments expanded dramatically.

Queen Juliana of the Netherlands ordered an exhibition of the ideas of the Club of Rome to be displayed in the center of Rotterdam. Soon after that the Club held meetings with the French minister of finance and put in place the so-called *Recontless International's* to discuss the implications of the Club of Rome's report.

CHAPTER 13

DIRE PREDICTIONS

I n 1972, Peccei was invited by the Council of Europe to present a paper called the "Limits of Growth in Perspective" before a special session of European parliamentarians.

In early 1974, thanks to the work done by Peccei and Austrian chancellor Bruno Krysky—Willy Brandt's Social Democratic friend—ten members of the Club of Rome held a private meeting with several heads of state, including former Prime Minister Pierre Trudeaux of Canada, Joop Den Uyl a former Prime Minister of the Netherlands, former president of the Swiss Confederation Nello Tiello, the representatives of Algeria and Pakistan and so on. In the words of Peccei, the seeds of doubt were sown.

The Forrester-Meadows report also triggered very extensive opposition from industrialists and other people who realized that zero-growth policies would never fit the United States of America. In consequence of that realization, an attempt was made by the Club to secure a counter-movement headed by M. Misarovick and Edward Pestell, who declared that the aim of the Club of Rome was programming organic growth:

"The world has a cancer and the cancer is man," said

Pestell.

Then the COR called for the development of a master plan leading to the creation of a new mankind, in other words, a New World Order run by these people.

The Club of Rome was to move into several Third World countries, including Iran, Egypt and Venezuela, Mexico and Algeria, after which they were invited to join, but declined do so.

A blueprint of the United Nations Institute of Training and Research called *Projects of the Future*, by Club of Rome member Irvin Lazlow was merely a bitter denunciation of industrial growth and urban civilization. He denounced the present policies of industrialization of the United States of America. He denounced the middle class and he demanded, as Lenin did before him, the total destruction of the American middle class, that unique institution, that organism, that keeps the United States from going the way of the Greek and Roman empires.

In this, Lazlow was ably helped by COR paid servants, Cyrus Vance and Henry Kissinger. Many of the Socialists named in this monograph met regularly with Vance and Kissinger.

As I mentioned in an earlier work, the Club of Rome sponsored a project to rewrite the book of Genesis, to replace the Bible's injunction that man has dominion over nature.

Other sympathizers of the Club of Rome included Cyrus Vance and Jimmy Carter himself, as well as Sol Linowitz,

Phillip Klutznick, William Ryan—of the Jesuit Order out of Toronto and Peter Henriatt, who was a liberation theology expert.

These people all met under the auspices of the Club of Rome in order to promote a world-wide campaign of religious fundamentalism that could be used to subvert world order and existing governments when the time is right, and that plan is a work in progress. It is partially in place, but as yet not fully developed.

I would like to return to the question of nuclear energy. There is tremendous pressure against nuclear energy—and we have seen action on all fronts; judicial, economic, social and political. But according to studies conducted at West Germany's Arken University covering the effects of nuclear weapons, if only 10 percent of the nuclear weapons of the super powers were detonated, the by-product would include a very significant amount of Cesium isotope, which, it was projected, would be assimilated into the iodine track within the living process. Sufficient enough such radioactive Cesium could be generated to kill all higher forms of life affected by it throughout the entire world.

But this of course is just another sheer horror story put out by the Club of Rome, just as the fear of a thermonuclear war is a horror story manipulated by the brain-washers on both sides of the Atlantic.

The idea behind it is to make the very name "radioactive" a horror word in the minds of people in the majority of the world's population. Thus the fear generated against the peaceful use of nuclear energy, has been very, very strong and has successfully subverted a number of significant construction plans and put on hold, scores of nuclear power plants that were to be built in the United States during the next ten years.

The only danger which gives nightmares to some honest people, is the fear that either a nuclear plant might be hit by a powerful nuclear explosion, or that some highly-trained anti-nuclear fanatic might penetrate the nuclear plant and blow it up, which, of course, would cause a secondary explosion.

However, attempted sabotage of nuclear plants as conclusive evidence proved at Three Mile Island is not likely to do anything near the damage that would be caused by detonation of nuclear weapons.

Lives are in jeopardy right now from scores of man-made viruses like HIV and Ebola Fever, in which nuclear energy plays no part whatsoever.

The study, using standard techniques, showed that even by the most conservative estimates, more than 1 million jobs were lost through elimination of nuclear energy installations already committed for construction and those already operating in the middle of 2008. Yet, not one single person has been killed by commercial fission energy generation in the United States! That is right; not one single person died in the so-called "nuclear disaster" at the Three Mile Island power station, which was not an accident, but a deliberately planned act of sabotage.

In the same time frame, millions have died of Aids, and millions more are going to die, thanks to the Global 2000 genocidal plans. Over 50,000 people die on the roads in

America in auto accidents **each year,** but so far, in more than four decades, nuclear power stations in the United States have not killed one single person!

But over 100 million lives have been jeopardized by the pro anti-nuclear Club of Rome and NATO forces, which are constantly brainwashing this nation with a barrage of antinuclear propaganda.

The interesting thing about it is this: The human body itself produces radioactivity to the point that prominent physicists a few years ago proposed that no more than two persons be allowed in the same room at one time. And another thing, a mountain ski trip or a flight in an airliner exposes a person to far more radioactivity than leaning against the wall of a nuclear power station for a year.

Another interesting point, a coal-burning plant gives off more radioactivity into the atmosphere per kilowatt, than a fission plant does. By mining uranium for fissionable fuel, we are actually reducing the total amount of radioactivity to which one is exposed through natural consequences.

At present, the existing programs of reprocessing and fractional waste disposal absolutely protect humanity from any risk whatsoever, on condition of course that the material is kept within the combustion reprocessing cycle. And it can be done.

Therefore the anti-nuclear fanatics, who have sabotaged this country's nuclear program, have been true to their denunciation of the accumulation of radioactive fuel wastes. With the coming on-line of breeder reactors the fractional amount of unprocessed waste, which is under five percent, can still be reduced further. By using the particle beam programs as invented and set up by the genius of Dr. Edward Teller, accelerated neutron beams can be applied to unwanted waste, and that could be completely neutralized by transforming it through controlled neutron bombardment. This has been done and can be done, and is fully practicable, and is certainly not costly.

Since the 1970's, we have seen the Club of Rome wage a tremendous war against nuclear energy programs in this country, which they have either killed outright through the fears of the environmentalists, or through withdrawing financing for these installations or a combination of both. All this has had the net effect of driving up by billions of dollars, the costs of construction of the nuclear power plants, and of course, the costs of eventually generating energy from these plants.

A nuclear power plant is normally easy to complete within a matter of four years but of course, if the time of construction is doubled—such as has happened in America due to opposition from environmentalists, local and state government—the construction and financing charges send the final price of the plant zooming out of sight.

These costly delaying tactics combined with the Club of Rome banker's high interest rates, which amount to plain outright usury brought nuclear power plant construction to a virtual halt in the U.S., and it is more crucial in 2008 with the soaring prices of crude oil, that nuclear-fired power plants be built.

Antinuclear power generating stations have to be one of the great success stories on the books of the Club of Rome.

Were it not so, we would already have seen tremendous strides in the industrialization of America and I am moved to say that unemployment would be a thing of the past.

Right now, as we come to mid 2008, we have some 15 million Americans out of work, or so the government says. With nuclear power plants in full production it would not be so. Nuclear fuel is the lowest cost per kilowatt of any fuel available in the world, now or at any time.

CHAPTER 14

CURBING NUCLEAR ENERGY

Fusion technology is the only ecologically acceptable source of new energy required if, and this is a big if, the United States is to continue with a healthy economy and a growing industrial base providing full employment for its large pool of skilled workers. Without a healthy economy and without a growing industrial base, the United States cannot remain a world power or even maintain its present shaky position in the structure of world military power ratings. If we could defeat the plans of the Club of Rome there would be three immediate areas of benefit to the country as a whole:

> ➤ There would be a tremendous development of our economic infrastructure, which would launch the greatest economic boom the United States has ever seen.

> ➤ It would provide employment opportunities, wiping out, I venture to suggest, the entire unemployed base of the U.S.

> ➤ It would increase the profits of investors. It would also bring down and make less costly the production of energy in America, and this would not cost the economy one additional penny. Imagine the benefits of not having to import Saudi oil. Our balance-of—

payments situation would improve in leaps and bounds. In six months our economy and job market will have undergone a startling transition.

All this would be done without increasing taxes. The technology is there and the will is there—what stands in the way of national development is the Club of Rome with its orchestrated policy of opposition towards nuclear energy.

Therefore, it is up to us to spread the message that nuclear energy is not evil, but good. If somehow, we had representatives in Congress who would put the United States first, and not their own interests, a nuclear energy program could be launched that would bring a new boom in high technology investment with millions of dollars invested and hundreds of thousands of new jobs created.

We would see new industries spring up; we would see unemployment vanish and the living standard of this country would be raised immeasurably and our industrial base and economic base would provide the incentive to make us the strongest military power in the world.

We would never again have to be concerned about an attack by a foreign power and never again experience the boom/bust cycles of prosperity and depression, forced upon the United States by the Federal Reserve banks.

This is, of course, diametrically opposed to the policies of the Club of Rome. Therefore, we are in a fight for our very future, for our very lives, for our children, and for the safety of this great country, the last bastions of freedom in the world. What has led to our present state of recession? And don't let government statistics fool you; we are in the throes of a deep recession.

What has brought us to this sorry pass? Have the natural resources of this country crumbled? Surely by now, the bulk of the population must realize that events do not simply happen, but are created through careful planning. At the root cause of the illness which besets America is the failure of successive governments, following that of President Roosevelt, to insist that Britain treat the United States as a separate, independent, sovereign country, instead of imposing the will of the Committee of 300 through the Club of Rome and the International Monetary Fund upon this country as they have done since the special agreement entered into by Winston Churchill and F. D. Roosevelt in 1938.

Of course the "special agreement" began long before that. Some people have written to me to say, "You must be wrong, as Churchill wasn't even the Prime Minister of England in 1938."

Certainly, but since when do these people worry about titles? When the infamous Balfour Treaty was accepted, did these people go to the Prime Minister of England, who was ostensibly in control of Britain? No, they submitted instead a lengthy memorandum to Lord Rothschild, and it was Lord Rothschild who did the final drafting of the treaty that gave away Palestine to the Zionists, which Britain had no right to give, as it did not belong to them.

We found the same thing happening with Roosevelt and Churchill. Churchill was not the prime minister in 1938, but that did not stop him negotiating on behalf of the people who owned him, body and soul; the **Committee of 300.**

Churchill received his training in the Boer War in South Africa, and he was always a member and messenger of this elite group for his entire lifetime.

Some indication of the type of strategy adopted by Britain is provided in the book published at the end of WWII by Elliot Roosevelt, son and wartime aide to Franklin Roosevelt entitled, *As I Saw It.*

Elliot Roosevelt documented the key features of Franklin Roosevelt outlining U.S. post war policy to Churchill. Of course, Churchill had no intention of following it; he knew very well, that the power to subvert whatever proposals Roosevelt made, lay with the Committee of 300 that runs America.

British Socialist agents of change infiltrated the United States by the score, including Walter Lippmann, who was the top propagandist at Tavistock. It was Lippman who introduced Lord John Maynard Keynes, the "marvelous" economist to an unsuspecting America, and it was Keynesian economic that ruined the economy of the U.S.

It was Keynes who introduced schemes like special drawing rites, the "multiplier" theory, and other grotesquely immoral, wicked, vile injustices imposed upon almost the entire human race by the small minority that runs the world. And we need to realize that this is no empty phrase. These people do indeed run the world and it is useless to say, "… this is America and we have a Constitution and it can't happen here."

The Constitution of the United States has been trampled under foot and has been totally and thoroughly subverted, so that today it is almost of no force and effect whatsoever.

Rockefeller created the Foreign Aid scam. It is the biggest rip-off the world has ever seen outside of the Federal Reserve banks. It makes nations entirely dependent on the dole, on handouts from the United States, which has a two-fold purpose:

> ➢ It keeps these nations subservient to the will of their masters in the Council on Foreign Relations.

> ➢ It taxes the United States tax payer beyond his capacity to pay and keeps him so busy earning a living just keeping his head above water, that he has no time to look around to see what is causing his misery. This scheme began in 1946.

Kissinger introduced hooliganism into world politics. Julius Klein of the OSS gave Kissinger his army job as General Kramer's driver. Kissinger has acted like a hooligan in world politics ever since the British took him over and has cost the American image and the public dearly.

It is mainly the work of Kissinger that brought on the agony of the starving millions in Africa and which has caused nations to bend and hand over their sovereign integrity.

It is amazing, and could never have happened three or four years ago, but it is happening right now, under our very noses in Brazil, Mexico and Argentina, where the IMF, the illegal organization of the One World Government, the bastard child of the Club of Rome, is forcing nations to bow the knee and hand over their sovereign integrity and their raw materials or be bankrupted.

This One World international bank was set up to rob, strip, and denude every weak country of its natural resources. This is what the IMF is all about. The IMF is one of the key factors in the Club of Rome's ability to dominate so many nations.

Now, I don't believe that I am better informed than those Senators and Congressmen in Washington and I don't earn anything like their salaries, yet these so-called representatives of We, the People, support unconstitutional funding of the bandit International Monetary Fund, which will eventually, take over the credit and monetary policies of the United States, thereby enslaving the people in a One World Government state.

Our representatives—*if they ever were our representatives*—could bring order and stability back to the United States by the stroke of a pen, if only we had even a handful of legislators who would be willing to obey the Constitution. We could begin a new industrialization of this country by abolishing the Federal Reserve Board; by deciding upon an equitable system of distribution and by bringing in nuclear power, not only into this country, but into all developing countries.

I believe we would embark on a period of Utopia for this world, such as we have never seen before. That, of course is entirely at variance with the plans of the Club of Rome, not only for this country, but also for the rest of the world.

There are several interesting aspects of the work of the Club of Rome, one, as I have previously mentioned, being the Global 2000 genocidal plan, which is based on the Draper Fund Population Crisis Committee report, supported by

Gen. Maxwell Taylor and others in the military.

For those of you who have asked me about certain people in the military, I suggest you ask them whether they support the Draper Fund Population Crisis Committee's findings and the Global 2000 genocidal report.

Gen. Taylor starts from the ridiculous presumption from which the Malthusians all start, wealth being derived from natural resources. Gen. Taylor argues that the population of the developing nations consumes too large a portion of raw materials, which will be needed for the elite in the coming centuries.

CHAPTER 15

GLOBAL 2000 REPORT

Therefore, the argument goes, we must act now to keep consumption as low as possible by cutting off technology and keeping food in short supply.

We must be prepared to let Third World populations starve, so that their country's raw materials are not absorbed by their nationals, but are available for the rulers of the world.

That is the underlying premise of the Global 2000 Report and Gen. Maxwell Taylor's Draper Fund Population Crisis Committee. It is not surprising to find Robert McNamara was involved in that type of rationale.

After all, we know very well the role McNamara played in Vietnam and we know perhaps less well, the role-played by the Club of Rome in formulating a policy of genocide, which was carried out by the Pol Pot regime in Cambodia.

That plot was hatched and set in motion in Cambodia as an experiment. And don't think that the same thing couldn't happen in America; it can and it will. Taylor and McNamara were great proponents of deploying NATO outside of theater (Europe) in violation of its Charter to operate only in Europe.

In other words, using NATO troops, recalcitrant nations will be coerced into paying their usury-debts to the IMF, under threat of an invasion. That is really the bottom line of the whole thing, a threat against civilized conduct.

Our civilization and our heritage are at stake; handed down by the solons of Athens and the Ionian city-state republics so that we can trace the impulse to govern, our Christian ideals, and two of the features of Christianity being central to this ideal.

We must govern ourselves by the book of Genesis, "be fruitful, multiply and fill the Earth and subdue it." We can increase and sustain human life and make it excellent and far better than it is now. Not for the few, who know the esoteric rules and the secret laws of cultism and occultism, but for the majority, the great majority whom Christ said He came to make free, and again I use this strictly in a non-religious context.

We must govern ourselves under the influence of the Christian principles, exemplified by Christ, by perfecting His rational powers of mind and expressing His faith in God, a living God, who will always treat human life as sacred.

We must not allow these occult black magic artists to trick us into believing that humanity is a mass of people. That is a lie. Humanity is not a mass; the very idea that each of us is an individual is brought out by the fact that we have individual sets of fingerprints.

There are no two sets of fingerprints alike in the whole world. Therefore, we are not a mass of people, we are individuals. We must gather technological information and put it to good use before the Club of Rome reduces us to a babbling troop of easily managed sub-humans, totally dependent on them for a hand-out and for our very existence, which promises to be very meager.

Any head of a nation who accepts the cult of the Club of Rome's Malthusian policies, which simply stated means that only a few must benefit at the expense of the many, has doomed himself and his people to a thousand years of slavery.

Under Malthusian restraints, no nation can expand or grow because if it does, it will use up the natural resources that the Club of Rome says belong to the few, the ruling class. Such a nation is doomed to perish because the evil influences that follow such a policy cannot survive in the light of day.

This is what is behind the so-called "conditionalities" imposed by the IMF on Brazil and Mexico. The IMF actually wants those nations to remain poor.

Therefore, it makes conditions for loans so impossible to comply with, that nations burn themselves out simply trying to repay the interest. Thereby, they hand themselves over, body and soul, to the dictates and control of the IMF, which as I have said, is the financial arm of the Club of Rome. We must not stand by and allow these things to happen.

The Club of Rome is fully aware, even if our people are not, that every successful 19th century industrial country except for Britain, was motivated by the American system of political economy and yet, no university in America teaches this today. They are afraid to teach it.

Socialists Professor Laski of the Fabian Society forbad it. But we see it before our very eyes—only in Japan is the American system still successfully applied. This accounts for the apparent superiority of the Japanese economy vis-a-vis that of America. We were forced to abandon our own American political economy system in favor of the Black Nobility's idea of how things ought to be run, which is world Socialism in action.

But Japan baulked. The performance of the Japanese economy is proof positive that the American system works if given a chance. But the U.S. has this cancer upon its society called the Club of Rome, which is blocking government, blocking our legislatures, blocking progress in the nuclear energy field, destroying our steel mills, our auto industry and our housing industry, while the Japanese are forging ahead. Of course, they too are slated for a big setback and as soon as the Club of Rome feels strong enough, it will turn its attention to the Japanese who will suffer the same fate.

We must not allow this to happen. We must fight to keep America a civilized, industrial nation. We must find leaders who will once again follow the policies of George Washington and in so far as political economy is concerned, cast out the likes of Keynes, Laski, Kissinger and the Bush family who have brought this country to the point of ruination, which is just about the point of ruination "… Yes! We're on the eve of destruction."

History teaches that Christianity emerged as an institutional force in opposition to the powers of darkness. Christ said,

"I come to give you light and freedom."

He was speaking to the people who at the time were considered nothing but the scum of the Earth by the elite minority.

CHAPTER 16

THE BLACK NOBILITY

Christianity produced the most powerful form of civilization in the matter of state policy and culture, which is why the Club of Rome is so bitterly opposed to the Christian doctrine. As far as I know the last effort to create a single state of Western Christendom was defeated around 1268 A.D. by the Venetian—directed Black Guelph who defeated the forces associated with Alighieri Dante, the great Italian poet.

Many attempts were made in Europe to make a new kind of state. The sovereign nation state republic is based on shared usage of common language, replacing dialects, which were prevalent at that time. Dante's design was good and it stood very well until it was defeated, which we know was as a direct result of crushing the republic forces in England through the 1603 establishment of the British monarchy under the direction of the Venetian puppet, James I. When I say James I, Venetian puppet, I am talking about the Black Nobility.

We know that because of this, every effort was made to crush this new form of nation state republicanism. That war is still going on today. The American War of Independence has never ended. It has been an ongoing "battle" from 1776, and since then America has lost two major battles:

In 1913 we were defeated by two acts of the Federal Government in the imposition of a graduated income tax— a Marxist doctrine—and the imposition of the Federal Reserve banks, a privately owned banking monopoly.

But even before that, terrible blows were delivered to the American Republic through the passage of the "specie resumption act" in 1876–1879, when the United States surrendered its sovereignty over its national credit currency and debt policies and placed the monetary policies of the young Republic at the mercy of the international merchants of the gold exchange in London. Internal power over our monetary affairs was thereafter increasingly at the beck and call of the powerful agents of the British and Swiss bankers via August Belmont, a relative of the Rothschilds who sent him to the U.S. to front for their interests, and the J.P. Morgan dynasty.

Although the London gold exchange system itself collapsed in successive phases over the span between World Wars I and II, the Anglo-Swiss Venetian Fondi, that is to say the people with the funds, established a virtual dictatorship over the world's monetary affairs under the Bretton-Woods agreement, the swindle of the century.

The United States has the power to destroy all those chains that bind its people; it can, and it could, if only we could elect legislators who would place their country ahead of their own personal interests and set about destroying this monstrosity of Socialism, which has us by the throat, which we now call the Club of Rome.

Several people have asked me, "If what you say is true, why is it that our universities and schools don't teach the type of economics that you're talking about?"

Let me point out that lengthy centuries of dictatorship of London and the Swiss bankers over the world's monetary system and affairs is the absolute number one reason why no U.S. university's economic department or schools teach proper economics or uphold the bimetallism monetary system on which our Republic, the United States of America was based and which made the United States the richest and best run country in the world.

If real economics were taught, Socialism would go out the window. Students would see exactly what is wrong with this country and begin to search for where to lay the blame.

As long as we, as a nation, allow unlawful subversion of our sovereignty through political and economic decision making and we subordinate ourselves to supranational monetary institutions such as the IMF and the Bank of International Settlements, as long as the American Bar Association, "our" lawyers, "our" government, "our" congressmen and "our" private sector economy continue to please these subversive monetary agencies, these supra national financial institutions, just as long will our country go to wrack and ruin.

We should not have to please any supranational institution, or play by the rules that they wish to dictate to us. Just recently, we have seen again how Congress has gone along with the evil scheme of bailing out this despicable Laski-Keynes-Socialist inspired institute called the International Monetary Fund.

We need to teach our people exactly what is going on with

the IMF and the Club of Rome. Economics is not a subject that is really all that complicated. Once one grasps the principles, it is fairly easy to follow. Let me just give you some examples of how we have been betraying ourselves by allowing the dictates of the Socialist international supranational organizations that have imposed themselves upon our nation like a cancer.

Take the immediate post WWII war period; some 62 percent of our national labor force was employed in either the production of tangible goods or the transportation of those goods. Today, if we use the official statistics—which are highly unreliable at the best of times—less than 30 percent of our labor force is employed at this level. Unemployment is in the region of 20 percent. The shift in the composition of employment of the national labor force is the underlying cause of inflation. That is principally where the trouble lies.

If we look at history, especially of the 1870's, we observe a general lessening of costs of producing goods, a deflationary cycle in the advance of the production of wealth, caused chiefly by the influence of the American system of political economy, in fostering technological progress in the form of industrial progress and the rise in agricultural productivity. But from the take-over of the world's monetary affairs by the London gold exchange system held in the hands of a few during the 1880's, hideous depressions have followed one another in rapid succession and in between we have seen long spirals of inflation.

This has been a direct product of the Malthusian forces that control this world who were associated with the doctrines of John Stewart Mill, Harold Laski and John Maynard Keynes. The policies of so-called economic freedom of the market place do nothing but increase the speculative investments in fictitious rent capitalization's and renter financier forms of usury at the expense of investments in true technology and true progressive production of real and tangible goods.

That is why I tell all my friends, "stay away from the stock market." The stock market is a fictitious area of speculative investment, and it is not an area where money is invested in technological progress for the production of tangible goods in a progressive and orderly manner.

Therefore, the stock market must collapse. It cannot be propped up forever nor hold itself up forever. It is a bubble of hot air, which will be pricked and when that happens, many are going to be hurt.

The trick is to get people to listen now before it happens. At the behest of the Club of Rome, the flow of credit has shifted away from production of goods and agricultural production towards non-goods-producing forms of financial investment. Of course this has created tremendous problems for the country.

The shift in the composition of financial flows and employment was the cause of both periodic major depressions and long term inflationary movements built inside what is now our economic system. I did not intend this to turn into an exposition of economic facts, but sometimes it is necessary to bring these things to our attention. There is an evil force at work in America today, and it is called Socialism, on whose behalf the Club of Rome acts.

It is a body dedicated to the destruction of the United States of America, as we know it. It is a body dedicated to ushering in the New World Order in which the so-called privileged few, the **Committee of 300,** will rule.

Our fate will surely be decided unless we can muster men of good will and force a change in the policies of our government. This can only come about by cleaning house, cleaning the Augean stables, and getting rid of such secret organizations as the Club of Rome, so that they are longer able to dictate the course of events and control the future of this great country. Unless and until we do that, we are headed for slavery in a One World Government-New World Order.

Other titles

OMNIA VERITAS LTD PRESENTS:

BEYOND the CONSPIRACY
UNMASKING THE INVISIBLE WORLD GOVERNMENT

by John Coleman

All great historical events are planned in secret by men who surround themselves with total discretion.

Highly organized groups always have the advantage over citizens

OMNIA VERITAS LTD PRESENTS:

ABORTION
GENOCIDE IN AMERICA

BY JOHN COLEMAN

I MAINTAIN THAT WHEN A WOMAN AGREES TO AN ABORTION IN A NON-LIFE THREATENING SITUATION, SHE HAS TAKEN LEAVE OF HER SENSES AND SHOULD BE ADJUDGED "TEMPORARILY INSANE."

ABORTION SHOULD BE EXPLAINED AS EUPHEMISM FOR "MURDER BY DECEPTION"

OMNIA VERITAS LTD PRESENTS:

DIPLOMACY BY DECEPTION
AN ACCOUNT OF THE TREASONOUS CONDUCT BY THE GOVERNMENTS OF BRITAIN AND THE UNITED STATES

BY JOHN COLEMAN

The story of the creation of the United Nations is a classic case of diplomacy by deception

OMNIA VERITAS LTD PRESENTS:

DRUG WAR against AMERICA

The drug trade cannot be eradicated because its directors will not allow the world's most lucrative market to be taken away from them...

BY JOHN COLEMAN

The real promoters of this cursed trade are the "elites" of this world.

OMNIA VERITAS LTD PRESENTS:

FREEMASONRY from A to Z

In the 21st century, Freemasonry has become less a secret society than a "society of secrets".

by John Coleman

This book explains what masonry is

OMNIA VERITAS LTD PRESENTS:

THE ROTHSCHILD DYNASTY

by John Coleman

Historical events are often caused by a "hidden hand"...

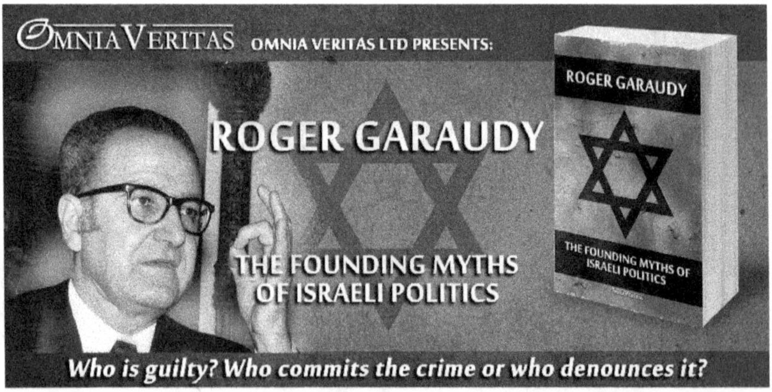
OMNIA VERITAS
OMNIA VERITAS LTD PRESENTS:
ROGER GARAUDY
THE FOUNDING MYTHS OF ISRAELI POLITICS
ROGER GARAUDY
THE FOUNDING MYTHS OF ISRAELI POLITICS
Who is guilty? Who commits the crime or who denounces it?

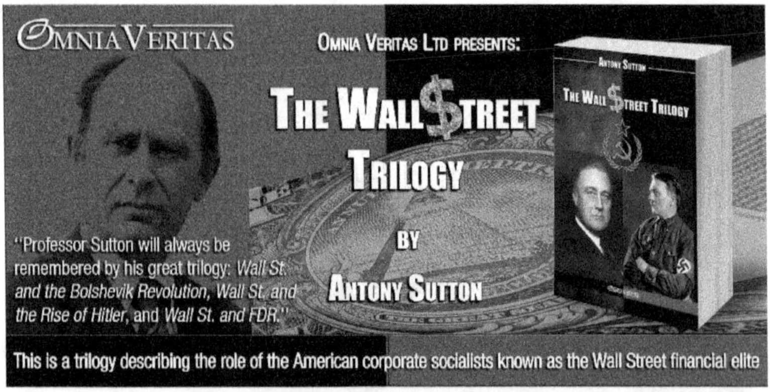
OMNIA VERITAS
OMNIA VERITAS LTD PRESENTS:
THE WALL $TREET TRILOGY
BY
ANTONY SUTTON
"Professor Sutton will always be remembered by his great trilogy: Wall St. and the Bolshevik Revolution, Wall St. and the Rise of Hitler, and Wall St. and FDR."
ANTONY SUTTON
THE WALL $TREET TRILOGY
This is a trilogy describing the role of the American corporate socialists known as the Wall Street financial elite

OMNIA VERITAS
Omnia Veritas Ltd presents:
HERVÉ RYSSEN
ISRAEL'S BILLIONS
Since time immemorial, spread in all countries, they are famous for having dedicated themselves to the great international trade. They are also, for centuries, the masters of banking and speculation.
HERVÉ RYSSEN
ISRAEL'S BILLIONS
Jews have a very particular relationship with money...

The "Jewish mafia", that one, does not exist; the Western media do not talk about it...

The cynicism and malice of these conspirators is something beyond the imagination of most Americans.

Only one people bas irritated its host nations in every part of the civilized world

Omnia Veritas Ltd presents:

THE CURSE OF CANAAN

A demonology of history

by

EUSTACE MULLINS

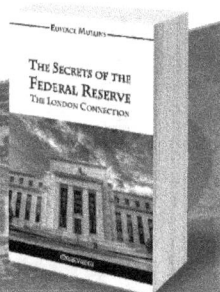

Liberalism, more popularly known as secular humanism, can be traced in an unbroken line all the way back to the Biblical "Curse of Canaan."

Humanism is the logical result of the demonology of history

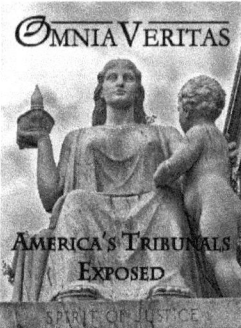

Omnia Veritas Ltd presents:

THE RAPE OF JUSTICE

by

EUSTACE MULLINS

AMERICA'S TRIBUNALS EXPOSED

American should know just what is going on in our courts

Omnia Veritas Ltd presents:

THE SECRETS OF THE FEDERAL RESERVE

by

EUSTACE MULLINS

HERE ARE THE SIMPLE FACTS OF THE GREAT BETRAYAL

Will we continue to be enslaved by the Babylonian debt money system?

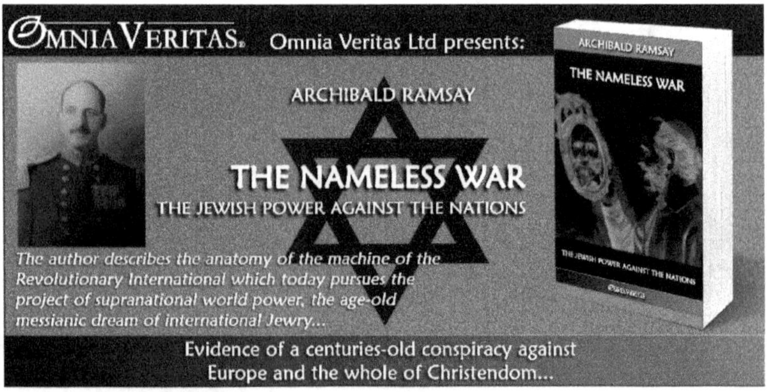
OMNIA VERITAS
Omnia Veritas Ltd presents:
ARCHIBALD RAMSAY
THE NAMELESS WAR
THE JEWISH POWER AGAINST THE NATIONS
The author describes the anatomy of the machine of the Revolutionary International which today pursues the project of supranational world power, the age-old messianic dream of international Jewry...
Evidence of a centuries-old conspiracy against Europe and the whole of Christendom...
ARCHIBALD RAMSAY
THE NAMELESS WAR
THE JEWISH POWER AGAINST THE NATIONS

OMNIA VERITAS
Omnia Veritas Ltd presents:
The Babylonian Woe
by
DAVID ASTLE
"There was a class of persons who very well understood each other's interests, who very likely were related by racial and religious custom, and whose supra-nationalism transcended all city boundaries and borders of states."
"Yesterday it was a conspiracy against the men of a city, or a relatively small state; today a conspiracy against the whole world."
The Babylonian Woe
David Astle's masterpiece in a brand new edition!

OMNIA VERITAS
Omnia Veritas Ltd presents:
FREDERICK SODDY
THE ROLE OF MONEY
WHAT IT SHOULD BE CONTRASTED
WITH WHAT IT HAS BECOME
This book attempts to clear up the mystery of money in its social aspect
FREDERICK SODDY
THE ROLE OF MONEY
WHAT IT SHOULD BE CONTRASTED WITH WHAT IT HAS BECOME
This, surely, is what the public really wants to know about money

www.ingramcontent.com/pod-product-compliance
Lightning Source LLC
Chambersburg PA
CBHW072204270326
41930CB00011B/2531